Make games with Python, 2nd Edition

Raspberry Pi Essentials: *Make Games with Python*, 2nd Edition
by Sean M. Tracey
ISBN: 978-1-916868-46-5
Copyright © 2025 Sean M. Tracey
Published by Raspberry Pi Ltd, 194 Science Park, Cambridge, CB4 0AB

Raspberry Pi Ireland Ltd, 25 North Wall Quay, Dublin 1, D01 H104
compliance@raspberrypi.com

Editor: Brian Jepson
Copy Editors: Phil King and Nicola King
Interior Designer: Sara Parodi
Production: Brian Jepson
Photographer: Brian O Halloran
Illustrator: Sam Alder
Graphics Editor: Natalie Turner
Publishing Director: Brian Jepson
Head of Design: Jack Willis
CEO: Eben Upton

July 2025: Second Edition
January 2016: First Edition

The publisher, and contributors accept no responsibility in respect of any omissions or errors relating to goods, products or services referred to or advertised in this book. Except where otherwise noted, the content of this book is licensed under a Creative Commons Attribution-NonCommercial-ShareAlike 3.0 Unported (CC BY-NC-SA 3.0).

Table of Contents

v   **Welcome**
vii   **About the author**

Chapter 1
1   Draw Shapes and Paths
Learn the basics of Pygame by drawing some simple lines and shapes

Chapter 2
17   Animate Shapes and Paths
Move shapes around the screen — in different directions and patterns, and at different speeds

Chapter 3
31   Take control: keyboard, mouse, and gamepad
Write some code to get to grips with the keyboard, mouse, and gamepad in Python and Pygame

Chapter 4
47   Your first game
Now that we've covered making shapes, animating them, and setting up control mechanisms, we have everything we need to make our first proper game

Chapter 5
65   Pygame Soundboard
Learn about loading and playing sounds in your Pygame projects by making a fun farmyard soundboard

Chapter 6
79   Physics and forces
Let's give our game objects mass and simulate the effects of gravity on their movements

Chapter 7
97   **Physics and Collisions**
What happens when a not-so-unstoppable force meets a not-so-immovable object? Let's create circles which bounce off one another

Chapter 8
113   **Fred's Bad Day**
Have your own bad day in this pulse-pounding sprite-powered barrel-dodging game

Chapter 9
129   **The Aliens Are Trying to Kill Me!**
Let's make the first half of our final game project, putting to use everything we've learned so far

Chapter 10
143   **The Aliens Are Here and They're Coming in Waves!**
To wrap up this book, we're going to give the space shooter game we started in the last chapter some extra polish

Welcome

While millions of us enjoy nothing more than spending hours racking up high scores on our favourite video games, too few are exposed to an even more gratifying way to spend time — making them.

In this book, you'll learn how to develop games with Python and Pygame, a Python library that accelerates game development. As you work through the examples and projects in this book, you'll better understand the games you play, and you'll also build the skills needed to create games of your own.

This book isn't aimed at complete programming beginners, but you don't need to be a Python expert. If you've written some simple programs in Python (or in a similar programming language), you'll have a good head start. It will also be helpful if you're comfortable working with GitHub repositories, and don't mind using the command line for basic administrative tasks. That said, command line expertise is not strictly necessary — as long as you are comfortable creating files and navigating your computer's file system, then you're ready to get started.

You'll soon find that coding your own shoot-'em-up game is infinitely more satisfying than beating any end-of-level boss!

You can find example code and other information about this book, including errata, in its GitHub repository at **rpimag.co/pygamebookgit**. If you've found what you believe is a mistake or error in the book, please let us know by using our errata submission form at **rpimag.co/pygamebookfeedback**. We've tested the games and instructions in this book on the latest Raspberry Pi hardware and operating system, but they will also work on Windows, macOS, and Linux.

About the author

Sean calls himself a technologist, which is a fancy way of saying he still hasn't decided what he wants to do with technology — other than everything. Sean has spent his career trying to avoid getting 'proper' jobs, and as such has had a hand in making a variety of fun and interesting projects, including a singing statue of Lionel Richie, wearable drum kits, chopstick bagpipes, time telling hats, and a life-sized Elvis Presley robot, to name only a few. You can follow his adventures at **smt.codes**.

Colophon

Raspberry Pi is an affordable way to do something useful, or to do something fun.

Democratising technology — providing access to tools — has been our motivation since the Raspberry Pi project began. By driving down the cost of general-purpose computing to below $5, we've opened up the ability for anybody to use computers in projects that used to require prohibitive amounts of capital. Today, with barriers to entry being removed, we see Raspberry Pi computers being used everywhere from interactive museum exhibits and schools to national postal sorting offices and government call centres. Kitchen table businesses all over the world have been able to scale and find success in a way that just wasn't possible in a world where integrating technology meant spending large sums on laptops and PCs.

Raspberry Pi removes the high entry cost to computing for people across all demographics: while children can benefit from a computing education that previously wasn't open to them, many adults have also historically been priced out of using computers for enterprise, entertainment, and creativity. Raspberry Pi eliminates those barriers.

Raspberry Pi Press

store.rpipress.cc

Raspberry Pi Press is your essential bookshelf for computing, gaming, and hands-on making. We are the publishing imprint of Raspberry Pi Ltd. From building a PC to building a cabinet, discover your passion, learn new skills, and make awesome stuff with our extensive range of books and monthly magazine.

Raspberry Pi Official Magazine

magazine.raspberrypi.com

Raspberry Pi Official Magazine is written for the Raspberry Pi community. It's packed with Raspberry Pi-themed projects, computing and electronics tutorials, how-to guides, and the latest community news and events.

Chapter 1

Draw Shapes and Paths

Learn the basics of Pygame by drawing some simple lines and shapes

In this book, we are going to learn to make Python games with Pygame. Pygame is designed to make it easy to create games and interactive software. We'll look at drawing, animation, keyboard and mouse controls, sound, and physics. Each chapter will add to our knowledge of Python game development, allowing us both to understand the games we play, and to create almost anything our imaginations can come up with.

This book isn't for absolute programming beginners, but it's not far from it: we're going to assume that you've written some simple Python (or similar) programs in the past and are able to create files and get around your computer's file system without too much difficulty.

Installing Python and Pygame

Both Python and Pygame are installed on Raspberry Pi OS by default. If you're running macOS or Windows, you'll need to install Python from **python.org/downloads**. Mac users can also use Homebrew (**brew.sh**) to install Python and many other packages. Python3 should be installed by default on most recent Linux distributions.

On macOS, Linux, or Windows, you'll first need to set up a *virtual environment* (a Python sandbox for installing libraries without affecting your Python installation). If you want to run the most recent version of Pygame rather than the version packaged with Raspberry Pi OS, you'll need a virtual environment there as well. You can use the Linux instructions on a Raspberry Pi. The Linux instructions also apply to the Windows Subsystem for Linux (WSL).

On macOS or Linux, use these commands to create a **Pygame** virtual environment in the **.virtualenvs** subdirectory under your home directory:

1. Open a Terminal window and run the command `python3 -m venv ~/.virtualenvs/Pygame`
2. Activate the environment by running the following command: `source ~/.virtualenvs/Pygame/bin/activate`

> **WINDOWS TERMINAL AND POWERSHELL**
>
> Windows Terminal runs PowerShell by default, but you can configure it to run Command Prompt instead (click the downward-pointing arrow on the tab bar, choose **Settings**, go to the **Startup** section, change the **Default profile**, and click **Save**). You can use a virtual environment with PowerShell, but you'd need to modify PowerShell's execution policy, so we suggest using the Command Prompt for simplicity's sake.

On Windows, use these commands to create a **Pygame** virtual environment in the **Envs** subdirectory under your home directory:

1. Open a Command Prompt window and run the command `py -m venv %USERPROFILE%\Envs\Pygame`. If the `py` command is not found, replace it with `python3` or `python` and try again.
2. Activate the environment by running the following command: `%USERPROFILE%\Envs\Pygame\Scripts\activate`

After you've activated the environment, you'll need to install Pygame (you only need to do this once) with:

`pip3 install pygame`

Quick Tip

You must activate the environment each time you open a new Terminal or Command Prompt window in order for it to take effect.

To make sure Pygame is installed correctly, activate the environment as shown in step 2 and then run `python -m pygame.examples.stars`. You should see a moving starfield appear. You can close the window when you're done enjoying the splendours of the cosmos. If it doesn't work, please visit the Pygame wiki at **pygame.org/wiki/GettingStarted** for detailed installation instructions.

You can configure many code editors, such as Thonny and Visual Studio Code, to be aware of your virtual environment. This can help when you want to run a script from the editor but may also help if your editor checks the syntax for your code as you type.

If you're using Thonny, click the Python menu (which reads **Local Python 3** by default) in the lower right of the window, click **Configure Interpreter**, and then make sure **Local Python 3** is selected in the "**Which kind of interpreter**" dropdown. Next, click the **...** button to the right of the selected Python executable, and navigate to the **Pygame** virtual environment folder you created earlier, open the **bin** (macOS or Linux) or **Scripts** (Windows) folder, then double-click on the file named **activate** (macOS or Linux) or **python.exe** (Windows). On macOS or Linux, the **.virtualenvs** folder will be hidden, so you can type **~/.virtualenvs/Pygame/bin** in the file chooser to navigate to the folder.

In Visual Studio Code, make sure you've installed the Python extension from Microsoft (**rpimag.co/vscodepy**), and that you have a Python program (a file ending in **.py**) open. Click the **Python** menu in the lower-right of the status bar, and you should see a list of all virtual environments. Pick the one named Pygame. The Visual Studio Code Python extension automatically looks for virtual environments in a folder in your home directory: **.virtualenvs** on macOS and Linux and **Envs** on Windows.

Creating shapes & paths

In this chapter, we're going to look at drawing and colouring various shapes in a window. This isn't quite Grand Theft Auto V, admittedly, but drawing shapes is the first step in building just about anything.

To start off, open your preferred code editor, create a new file, insert the following code into it and save it as **hello.py**:

```python
import pygame
pygame.init()
clock = pygame.time.Clock()
window = pygame.display.set_mode((500, 400))
while True:
    for event in pygame.event.get():
        if event.type == pygame.QUIT:
            pygame.quit()
            raise SystemExit

    # Begin drawing statements
    pygame.draw.rect(window, (255, 0, 0), (0, 0, 50, 30))
    # End drawing statements

    pygame.display.update()
    clock.tick(60)
```

In your Terminal or Command Prompt window, run the command **python hello.py**. If all has gone well, a new window will have opened showing you a red square on a black background in the top-left corner of the window. If it doesn't work, make sure you activated your virtual environment (see "Installing Python and Pygame" on page 1). We've just created our first Pygame program; let's walk through it.

Understanding hello.py

The first two lines of our first program are very simple: all we've done is told Python that we want to use Pygame. **import pygame** loads all of the Pygame code into our script, so we don't have to write all of that code ourselves. **pygame.init()** tells Pygame that we're ready to start using it.

The third line defines a `clock` that we'll use later to maintain a consistent *frame rate*, expressed in frames per second (fps). Let's look at the fourth line: `window` represents the application window for our Pygame program; each parameter affects the application window's shape and size. Width always precedes height. `window` is also the object that we'll use to tell other lines of code the surface on which they should draw shapes and set colours.

When we create our `window`, we're calling the `set_mode()` function of Pygame's `display` module, which is responsible for how the game window behaves. We're passing a *tuple* to `set_mode()` to tell it how big we want our game window to be. In this case, the application window is 500 pixels wide by 400 pixels tall. If we pass numbers that are bigger, the game window will be bigger; if we pass numbers that are smaller, the game window will be smaller as shown in **Figure 1-1**.

> **TUPLE**
>
> A tuple such as `(400, 500)` is like a list, but unlike a standard list, a tuple's contents can't be changed (it's *immutable*). For example, lists support methods such as `append()`, and tuples do not. Lists are delimited with square brackets, for example `[400, 500]`.

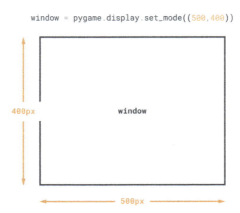

Figure 1-1 Each argument to `set_mode()` affects the application window's dimensions

The next few lines are where we make our program draw shapes on that window. When simple programs run, they execute their code, and when they're finished, they clean up after themselves. That's fine unless, of course, you want your program to be interactive, or to draw or animate shapes over time, which is exactly what we need from a game. So, to keep our program from exiting, we make a **while** loop and put all our code inside. The **while** loop will never finish because **True** is always **True**, so we can keep running our program and drawing our shapes for as long as we like.

The first thing we do in our **while** loop is check for any events, such as key presses, joystick motion, or even mouse actions. In this case, we're only checking for a **QUIT** event, which can be triggered by closing the window. If you quit the program in this way, the code will call Pygame's **quit()** function and will raise a **SystemExit** exception to terminate the Python program itself.

```
for event in pygame.event.get():
    if event.type == pygame.QUIT:
        pygame.quit()
        raise SystemExit
```

Next, we draw a rectangle each time through the loop. A rectangle is one of the simplest shapes that we can draw in Pygame:

```
pygame.draw.rect(window, (255, 0, 0), (0, 0, 50, 30))
```

The three arguments after **rect(** tell Pygame where to draw our rectangle (in the **window**), its colour, and its location and size. The first argument specifies the colour of our rectangle by representing how much red, green, and blue the colour should have in it. We use red, green, and blue because these are the three colours your screen combines to create every shade you can see on it. 0 means that none of that colour should be used; 255 indicates the maximum intensity of colour. We told our rectangle that it should be the colour **(255, 0, 0)**, which is pure red. If we had told it to be **(255, 0, 255)**, it would have been a bright purple, because it's being drawn with the maximum red and the maximum blue. If we had told our rectangle to be coloured **(100, 100, 100)**, it would be a dark grey, because all the colours would be equal.

> **LINE WIDTH**
>
> When drawing a rectangle or ellipse, you have the choice of passing a line width as the fourth argument. If you don't, the shape will be filled solid.

After we've passed in our rectangle's colour, we have to tell it where it should go and how big it should be. We do this by passing a tuple of four numbers. The first number is an X coordinate, which determines how far from the left side of the window to place the rectangle's left edge. The second number is a Y coordinate; this determines how far down from the top of our window to places the rectangle's top edge. The third number gives the width of our rectangle, and the fourth defines its height. So, for example, if we wanted our rectangle to be 50 pixels from the left side of the window, 100 pixels from the top of our window, 20 pixels wide, and 80 pixels tall, we would use **(50, 100, 20, 80)** as the third argument.

The next line in **hello.py** (**pygame.display.update()**) is simple: it tells Pygame that we're done drawing shapes for the moment and that it can now refresh the window. This saves Python having to draw and redraw the screen for every shape that we've created; instead, it can get them all drawn in one go. After that, we call **clock.tick(60)**, which makes sure the game runs at a consistent frame rate (60 fps) on different devices.

Adding more shapes

We've successfully drawn one shape, so let's draw a few more. We'll draw some squares around the screen and mess around with their properties a little bit. There's no need to create a new file, so we'll work with **hello.py** for now. Replace everything between the **# Begin** and **# End** comments so that section of code looks like this:

```
# Begin drawing statements
pygame.draw.rect(window, (255, 0, 0), (100, 100, 25, 25))
pygame.draw.rect(window, (0, 255, 0), (200, 150, 25, 25))
pygame.draw.rect(window, (0, 0, 255), (300, 200, 25, 25))
# End drawing statements
```

```
pygame.draw.rect(window,(255,0,0),(100,100,25,25))
pygame.draw.rect(window,(0,255,0),(200,150,25,25))
pygame.draw.rect(window,(0,0,255),(300,200,25,25))
```

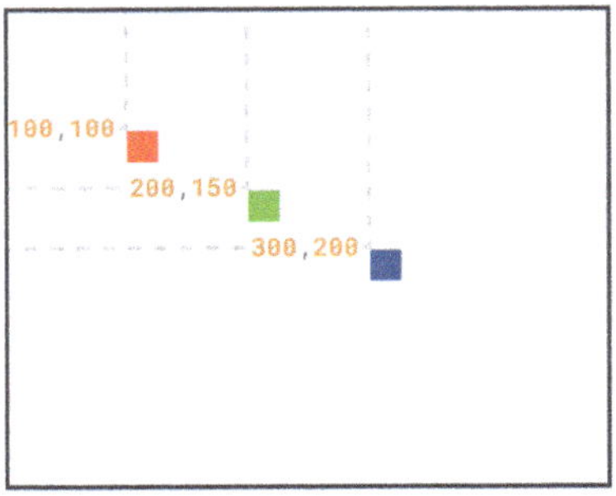

Figure 1-2 Setting shape attributes

Now we have three squares: red, blue, and green as shown in **Figure 1-2**. So far, this is nice and simple, but those squares have plenty of space between them. What would happen if they were to overlap? Let's find out. Change your code once more to the following:

```
# Begin drawing statements
pygame.draw.rect(window, (255, 0, 0), (0, 0, 50, 50))    # 1
pygame.draw.rect(window, (0, 255, 0), (40, 0, 50, 50))   # 2
pygame.draw.rect(window, (0, 0, 255), (80, 0, 50, 50))   # 3
# End drawing statements
```

This time we get two rectangles and a square, which is not what we asked for. So, what has gone wrong? Our code works through what it has to draw and where it has to put it, line-by-line. If one item is drawn and then another is drawn over it, the second shape obscures what is beneath it: some or all pixels of the first shape are lost when covered by another. To see this effect in action, swap the code for the second and third squares:

```
# Begin drawing statements
pygame.draw.rect(window, (255, 0, 0), (0, 0, 50, 50))    # 1
pygame.draw.rect(window, (0, 0, 255), (80, 0, 50, 50))   # 3
pygame.draw.rect(window, (0, 255, 0), (40, 0, 50, 50))   # 2
# End drawing statements
```

Now we get rectangle, square, rectangle because the red and blue squares were drawn first and then the green square was drawn over them. The red and blue squares are still there in their entirety, but we can't see all of them, so they look like rectangles.

Pygame allows us to do a great deal more than merely draw rectangles: we can make all kinds of other shapes too, including circles, ellipses, and paths (which are made up of many lines between multiple points).

Drawing circles

The process of drawing a circle is much like drawing a square except that, instead of passing a width and a height, we pass a radius and a point around which we draw our circle. For example, to draw a yellow circle with a diameter of 150 pixels, replace the code in the drawing section in **hello.py** with:

```
# Begin drawing statements
pygame.draw.circle(window, (255, 255, 0),
                   (250, 200), 75, 1)
# End drawing statements
```

Similar to drawing a rectangle, we tell Pygame on which surface to draw our circle, its colour, where it should go (200, 200), followed by its radius (75), and another argument (as illustrated in **Figure 1-3**).

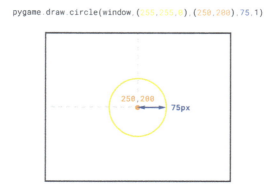

Figure 1-3 Drawing a circle

That final argument — the **1** that appeared after our radius — is a value used to determine the width of the line that draws our circle. If we pass **0**, the circle is filled; but if we pass **2**, for instance, we get a 2-pixel-wide line with an empty centre (see **Figure 1-4**):

```
# Begin drawing statements
# Filled
pygame.draw.circle(window, (255, 255, 0),
                   (200, 200), 20, 0)
# Not filled
pygame.draw.circle(window, (255, 255, 0),
                   (300, 200), 20, 2)
# End drawing statements
```

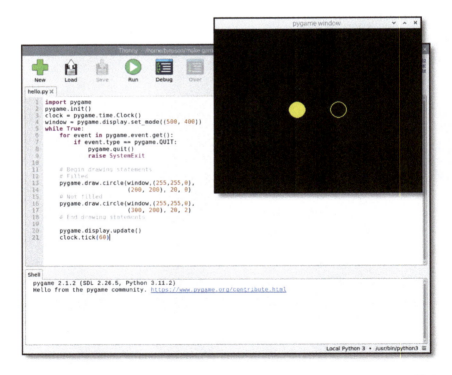

Figure 1-4   When drawing a circle, the last argument determines whether the circle should be filled

What about ellipses? They are a slightly strange cross between drawing rectangles and circles. As we did when we drew a rectangle, we pass an X coordinate, a Y coordinate, a width, and a height, but we end up with an elliptical shape. Let's draw some ellipses.

```
# Begin drawing statements
pygame.draw.ellipse(window, (255, 0, 0),
                    (100, 100, 100, 50))
pygame.draw.ellipse(window, (0, 255, 0),
                    (100, 150, 80, 40))
pygame.draw.ellipse(window, (0, 0, 255),
                    (100, 190, 60, 30))
# End drawing statements
```

Just as before, run your code. You should now see three ellipses: one red, one green, and one blue. Each should be a different size. If you wanted to visualise how these shapes were generated, you could draw rectangles using the same coordinates as you used to draw an ellipse and it would fit perfectly inside that box. As you may have guessed, this means you can also make circles by using **pygame.draw.ellipse()** if the width and height parameters are the same. **Figure 1-5** shows the result.

```
# Begin drawing statements
pygame.draw.rect(window, (255, 0, 0),
                 (100, 100, 100, 50), 2)
pygame.draw.ellipse(window, (255, 0, 0),
                    (100, 100, 100, 50))
pygame.draw.rect(window, (0, 255, 0),
                 (100, 150, 80, 40), 2)
pygame.draw.ellipse(window, (0, 255, 0),
                    (100, 150, 80, 40))
pygame.draw.rect(window, (0, 0, 255),
                 (100, 190, 60, 30), 2)
pygame.draw.ellipse(window, (0, 0, 255),
                    (100, 190, 60, 30))
#Circle
pygame.draw.ellipse(window, (0, 0, 255),
                    (100, 250, 40, 40))
# End drawing statements
```

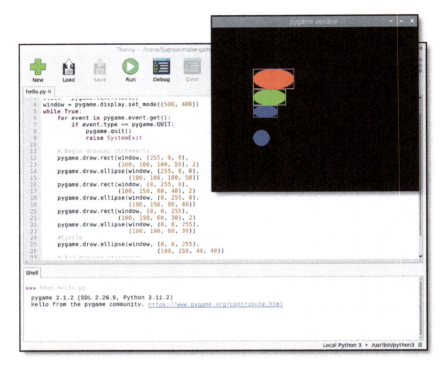

Figure 1-5 Ellipses in the rectangles that bound them

A new path

We have covered rectangles, squares and circles, but what if we want to draw a triangle, a pentagon, a hexagon, or an octagon? Unfortunately, there aren't functions for every kind of shape, but we can use paths. Paths allow us to draw irregular shapes by defining points in space, joining them up with lines, and filling in the space we've created. This is a little more complex, so it's time to move on from our original program. Create a new file, call it **paths.py**, and save it with the following text inside:

```
import pygame
pygame.init()
clock = pygame.time.Clock()
window = pygame.display.set_mode((500, 400))
```

```
while True:
    for event in pygame.event.get():
        if event.type == pygame.QUIT:
            pygame.quit()
            raise SystemExit

    # Begin drawing statements
    # End drawing statements

    pygame.display.update()
    clock.tick(60)
```

This is simply our bare-bones Pygame app again. If you want to make a copy of this for experimenting without breaking anything, now would be a good time to do so.

Every path is made of connected lines, but, before we start joining things up, let's draw a couple of standalone lines to familiarise ourselves with them. We can do this with `pygame.draw.line()`. Edit **paths.py** so your drawing statement section reads as follows:

```
    # Begin drawing statements
    pygame.draw.line(window, (255, 255, 255),
                     (0, 0), (500, 400), 1)
    # End drawing statements
```

If you run this code now, you'll see a one-pixel-wide white line going from the top left to the bottom right of our Pygame window. The arguments we pass to `pygame.draw.line()` start off the same way rectangles and ellipses do. We first tell Pygame where we want to draw the shape and then we choose a colour. After that, the arguments change a little. The next argument is a tuple with the X and Y coordinates for where we want our line to start, and the third argument is a tuple with the X and Y coordinates for where we want our line to end. These specify the two points between which our line will be drawn. The final argument is the width of the line being drawn in pixels.

With lines, we can now create shapes by defining points in our window. Let's draw that triangle we talked about earlier (see **Figure 1-6**):

```
# Begin drawing statements
pygame.draw.line(window, (0, 255, 0),
                 (150, 150), (225, 225), True)
pygame.draw.line(window, (0, 255, 0),
                 (225, 225), (75, 225), True)
pygame.draw.line(window, (0, 255, 0),
                 (75, 225), (150, 150), True)
# End drawing statements
```

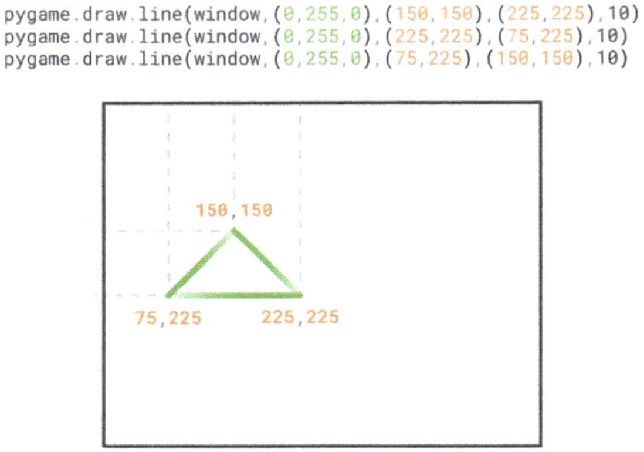

Figure 1-6   You can make a triangle from three separate lines

You should have an image of a green triangle with a 1px edge. However, this code is rather lengthy: so many things, like the colour or the width of the line, are written multiple times. There is, however, a more concise way to achieve the result we want. All we need is **pygame.draw.lines()**. Whereas **pygame.draw.line()** lets us draw a line between two points, **pygame.draw.lines()** enables us to draw a sequence of lines between numerous points. Each XY-coordinate point will be joined up to the next XY-coordinate point, which will be joined up to the next XY-coordinate point, and so on. You can see this in **Figure 1-7**.

```
pygame.draw.lines(window, (0, 255, 0), True,
                  ((150, 150), (225, 225), (75, 225)), 10)
```

```
pygame.draw.lines(window,(0,255,0),True,((150,150),(225,225),(75,225)),10)
```

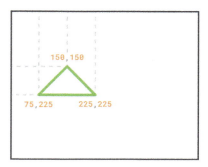

Figure 1-7 This triangle is made up of one line with multiple points

After running the code in the following listing, you'll see that the resulting triangle is exactly the same, except that we produced it from one line of code instead of three. You might have noticed that we didn't actually close the triangle: Pygame did it for us. Just before we pass the points for our shape to be drawn from, we can pass either a **True** or a **False** value that will let Pygame know that we want it to close our shapes for us. Change it to **False** and we get the first two lines of our shape, but not the third. If we want to make a more complex shape, we simply add more points like so:

```
# Begin drawing statements
pygame.draw.lines(window,(255, 255, 255), True,
                  ((50, 50), (75, 75), (63, 100),
                  (38, 100), (25, 75)), 1)
# End drawing statements
```

There you have it: your very own pentagon. If you want to make a hexagon, an octagon, or even a triacontagon, just add more points — it's that easy. Why not try experimenting with Pygame to produce some interesting pixel art?

Chapter 2

Animate Shapes and Paths

Move shapes around the screen — in different directions and patterns, and at different speeds

In Chapter 1, *Draw Shapes and Paths*, we looked at creating a variety of shapes in different sizes and colours. Now we're going to be looking at different ways of moving and manipulating those shapes over time. This chapter covers the fundamentals of moving shapes with code; Chapter 3, *Take control: keyboard, mouse, and gamepad* discusses using keyboard and mouse events to control how and when things move. In this tutorial, we won't be using one single Pygame program. Instead, we have a couple of different example programs, each demonstrating a different concept.

Moving shapes in time and space

When we think of animation, our minds might turn to cartoons and animated films where subtle changes in shape and colour trick our brains into seeing movement where there is none. It's no different with computers: whenever you move a mouse or minimise a window, nothing has actually been moved; instead, pixels have been drawn, updated, refreshed, and then drawn again, with everything in its new place.

Save the following program as **random_rect.py** and run it:

```
import pygame, random
pygame.init()
clock = pygame.time.Clock()

WIN_WIDTH = 640
WIN_HEIGHT = 480
window = pygame.display.set_mode((WIN_WIDTH, WIN_HEIGHT))
pygame.display.set_caption('Pygame Shapes!')

while True:
    for event in pygame.event.get():
        if event.type == pygame.QUIT:
            pygame.quit()
            raise SystemExit

    # Begin drawing statements
    window.fill((0,0,0))
    x = random.randint(0, WIN_WIDTH)
    y = random.randint(0, WIN_HEIGHT)
    pygame.draw.rect(window, (255,0,0), (x, y, 10, 10))
    # End drawing statements

    pygame.display.update()
    clock.tick(60)
```

> **Quick Tip**
>
> By default, our window is given the title 'Pygame window'. We can set that to anything we like, for example: **pygame.display.set_caption('Pygame Shapes!')**

If you run this program, you'll see a bunch of red squares appearing and disappearing all around the screen, as shown in **Figure 2-1**. Don't worry, nothing is broken! This is just to demonstrate Pygame drawing, destroying, and redrawing things in a window.

Add a **#** to the start of the line that starts **window.fill()**. We use this code to clear the pixel data from the previous frame. Without it, what we see is all of the different frames built up one on top of the other as time passes. **window.fill()** is like the paint that we use to cover old wallpaper before we add the new one: it creates a blank slate for us to work with.

Figure 2-1 A simulated screenshot showing the random placement of red squares in our window

But that's not very useful, is it? Remove the # you added, then add the following two lines before the `while True:` line:

```
green_square_x = WIN_WIDTH / 2
green_square_y = WIN_HEIGHT / 2
```

Next, replace the code between the # Begin and # End comments so that it reads like this:

```
# Begin drawing statements
window.fill((0,0,0))
pygame.draw.rect(window, (0, 255, 0),
                 (green_square_x, green_square_y, 10, 10))
green_square_x += 1
#green_square_y += 1
# End drawing statements
```

Save the modified file as **moving_square.py**, run it, and you'll see a green square moving to the right of the screen.

So, what's making the square move? In Chapter 1, *Draw Shapes and Paths*, we were drawing shapes like this using numbers that we would pass through to Pygame, as in `pygame.draw.rect(window, (0,255,0), (40, 0, 50, 50))`, and that's all well and good, providing you never want to change anything about that shape. What if we wanted to change the height, width, or colour of this shape? How could we tell Pygame to change the numbers that we've already entered? This is where variables come in. Rather than passing through numbers to `pygame.draw.rect()`, we pass in variables instead. After we've drawn the shapes, we can change the variable so that when it's next drawn, it will look slightly different (see **Figure 2-2**). Every time we draw our green square, we add 1 to the variable we use to define its X coordinate (how far it is from the left of the screen), `green_square_x`. We do this with `+=`, which basically says 'take the current value of the variable and then add whatever number comes after it'.

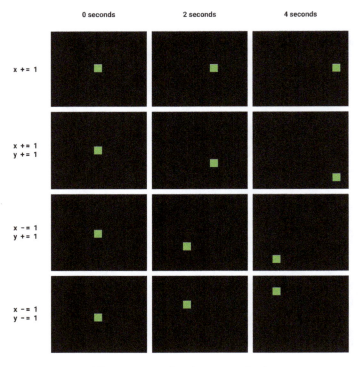

Figure 2-2 How different motions affect the position of a shape over time

If we change that line to read **green_square_x += 5**, every time we draw our square, it will be 5 pixels to the right of where it was the last time it was drawn. This gives the illusion of the shape moving faster than before. If we changed the number we add to **green_square_x** to 0, our shape would never move; and if we changed it to -5, it would move backwards.

Moving in all directions

So that's how we move left and right; if we can do that much, surely we can go up and down too? Comment out the **green_square_x += 1** line by adding a **#** before it and uncomment the line below by removing the **#**. Our square will start to travel towards the bottom of the screen. Just like before, we're changing the variable that tells our shape where to go, **green_square_y**, just a little bit each time to make it move. And, just as we saw by changing the X variable, we can make the green square go up by adding a negative number to its Y variable.

So now we can animate things moving in four directions; that's enough freedom to make so many classic games: Pokémon, Legend of Zelda, Space Invaders, and more. These games would only move things horizontally and vertically, but never at the same time. The next challenge would be how to make things move diagonally. Fortunately, this is a pretty simple process too.

If we uncomment both **green_square_x += 1** and **green_square_y += 1** in our code, then our shape will move to the right and down every time Pygame updates the screen. If we add to our X and Y values, our shape will move to the right and down. If we add to our X value and subtract from our Y value, then our shape will move to the right and up. If we subtract from our X value and add to our Y value, our shape will move to the left and down. Finally, if we subtract from both our X and Y values, our shape will move to the left and upwards. That means we have eight directions that our objects can move in (see **Figure 2-3**) — assuming, that is, that we use numbers that are equal to one another. If we used values that were different for our X and Y values, we'd have more variation. If we use floats (which are numbers with a decimal place, like 2.3 or 3.141) instead of integers (whole numbers), we could get a full 360 degrees of motion.

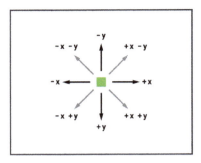

Figure 2-3 The eight basic directions a shape can move

So far, the values we've used to animate our shapes around the screen have been integers that remain constant. With each frame, we would always add 1 (or some other arbitrary value) to move our object. But what happens if we change the values that we use to animate things? What if, instead of adding 1 to X/Y coordinates, we add 1, then 1.1, then 1.2, and so on?

Replace the **green_square_x** and **green_square_y** lines above **while True:** with the following:

```
blue_square_x = 0.0
blue_square_y = 0.0
blue_square_vx = 1
blue_square_vy = 1
```

Next, replace the drawing statements with:

```
    # Begin drawing statements
    window.fill((0,0,0))
    pygame.draw.rect(window, (0, 0, 255),
                     (blue_square_x, blue_square_y, 10, 10))
    blue_square_x += blue_square_vx
    blue_square_y += blue_square_vy
    blue_square_vx += 0.1
    blue_square_vy += 0.1
    # End drawing statements
```

Save this new program as **moving_accel.py** and run it. What do you notice? We're adding to both our X and Y values, so our square is moving down and to the right, but something is different from our previous bits of code: as our program continues to run, our square moves to the right a little more than it did in the previous frames. It's accelerating. This is because we're using variables to represent the square's velocity, one each for the X and Y velocity. By gradually incrementing those variables, and adding them to our X and Y coordinates, we increase the amount of distance that is added in each frame, which gives the illusion of acceleration.

If changed our code so that it multiplied `blue_square_vx` and `blue_square_vy` by a number greater than one instead of using addition or subtraction, our shapes would accelerate much faster; we'd have hardly any time to see them before they ran off the screen.

Speaking of which, what happens to our shapes when they run off an edge and are no longer on our screen? Have they disappeared forever? The answer is no. You can think of our window like an actual window in your house, as shown in **Figure 2-4**. If you look out of the window to see a pedestrian who then moves further down the street so you can no longer see them, they haven't ceased to exist. They're just beyond your line of sight. If our shapes move further across our screen so that we can no longer see them, they don't stop moving or disappear, they keep on going for ever, or until you tell them to stop and come back.

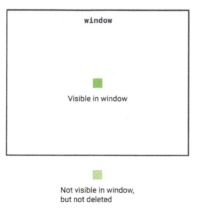

Figure 2-4 The box is the viewport of a Pygame window

Next, make the following changes:

1. Change the **blue_square_vx = 1** line to read **blue_square_vx = 8**
2. Change the **blue_square_vx += 0.1** line to **blue_square_vx -= 0.2**
3. Comment out the **blue_square_vy += 0.1** line

> **Quick Tip**
>
> If we want to subtract values from a variable, we don't always have to use **-=** for subtraction and **+=** for addition. We can use **+=** for both; simply add a negative number to take away numbers, for example: **4 + -3 = 1**.

Run it again, and you'll see that the square moves to the right across our screen, before slowing to a stop and then coming back on itself, forming an arcing animation, as shown in **Figure 2-5**. This is because the **blue_square_vx** variable has decreased to negative numbers, but the **blue_square_y** variable continues to increase.

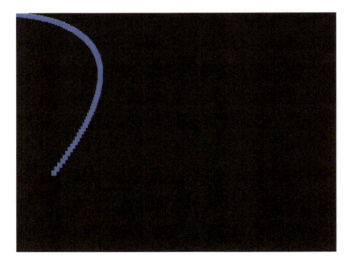

Figure 2-5 This is the path travelled by a shape moving across the window while accelerating

If we had subtracted the **vx** and **vy** variables in equal values, with equal starting speeds (both **vx** and **vy** being 8, for example), our shape would have continued along its path, stopped, and then reversed along the exact same path, with the same rate of acceleration as it slowed. Play with these values to see what effect they have on how our shape moves (see **Figure 2-6**). If you like, you can comment out the `window.fill()` line and you'll see the path our shape takes trailing behind it.

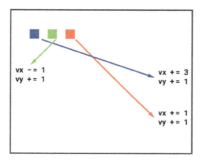

Figure 2-6 The varying effects of different acceleration values on shapes

Animating other properties

Animation isn't just about making things move: it's about making things change, too. Until now, we've been animating shapes by moving them, but we can use the same approach of changing variables over time to affect other properties, like the dimensions of our shapes. Replace the four lines you added above `while True:` with

```
rect_x = WIN_WIDTH / 2
rect_y = WIN_HEIGHT / 2
rect_width = 50
rect_height = 50
```

Next, replace the drawing statements with:

```
# Begin drawing statements
window.fill((0,0,0))
pygame.draw.rect(window, (255,255,0),
                (rect_x - rect_width / 2,
                 rect_y - rect_height / 2,
                 rect_width, rect_height))
```

```
    rect_width += 1
    rect_height += 1
    # End drawing statements
```

Save the program as **shape_change.py**. Here, `pygame.draw.rect` draws a rectangle just the same as we've done before, but, as in other examples, we've replaced the parameters that determine the width and height of our rectangle with variables that we change.

We also do a little bit of maths in our code (see **Figure 2-7**). As the square gets larger, the point from which it is drawn won't change, so the shape will get bigger, but it will do so off-centre from the rest of the window. By subtracting half of the width and half of the height from the coordinates that we draw our shape at, our square will remain in the centre of the window as it gets larger. The nice thing about using variables in our maths is that no matter how we change our variables, the shape created will always be in the centre of the window. Change the number on the `rect_width += 1` line to any other number between 2 and 10. Now, when our square enlarges, it becomes a rectangle, because its width increases faster than its height does, but it still remains in the centre.

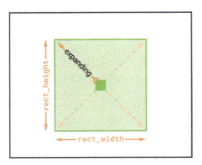

Figure 2-7   Keeping the square in the centre as it enlarges or shrinks

The same effect works in the opposite direction. If we start off with a square that has a width and a height of 50 and change the `+=` inside the `while` loop to `-=`, our square will decrease in size while remaining central to our window.

Changing colour over time

Just like our previous pieces of code, we're using variables in place of values to define what our shapes will look like with `pygame.draw.rect`. The next example, however, has something a little different from the previous examples. Here, we're not adding and subtracting values each and every time we draw our shapes; instead, we're checking the values that we have before we change them, using an `if-else` statement. For the chapter's final example, here's the code listing (**colour_change.py**) in its entirety:

```python
import pygame, random
pygame.init()
clock = pygame.time.Clock()

WIN_WIDTH = 640
WIN_HEIGHT = 480
window = pygame.display.set_mode((WIN_WIDTH, WIN_HEIGHT))
pygame.display.set_caption('Pygame Shapes!')

red_level = random.randint(0, 255)
green_level = random.randint(0, 255)
blue_level = random.randint(0, 255)

while True:
    for event in pygame.event.get():
        if event.type == pygame.QUIT:
            pygame.quit()
            raise SystemExit

    # Begin drawing statements
    window.fill((0,0,0))
    pygame.draw.rect(window,
                    (red_level, green_level, blue_level),
                    (50, 50, WIN_WIDTH / 2, WIN_HEIGHT / 2))
    if red_level >= 255:
        red_level = random.randint(0, 255)
    else:
        red_level += 1
    if green_level >= 255:
        green_level = random.randint(0, 255)
```

```
    else:
        green_level += 1
    if blue_level >= 255:
        blue_level = random.randint(0, 255)
    else:
        blue_level += 1
    # End drawing statements

    pygame.display.update()
    clock.tick(60)
```

This is a key concept of game development: a game's response to a player's actions is the result of hundreds and thousands of these little checks going on every few milliseconds. Without them, there would be no kind of order to any game: it would be like our first bit of code, with the square simply appearing and disappearing at random positions, and there's not much fun in that! With these **if-else** checks, we're making sure that the red, green, and blue values never go over 255 (the maximum value — Pygame will return an error if you specify greater than 255 or less than 0).

If a colour value is about to go over 255, we assign it a random value between 0 and 255. The colour of our square will change and will then continue to slowly work its way through the RGB colour palette by adding 1 to our R, G, and B variables (**red_level**, **green_level**, and **blue_level**) as our Pygame program runs. Just as before, if we added a larger number to each of our variables, we would cycle through the available colours more quickly. Similarly, if we added less to each RGB value every time Pygame updates, we would cycle through all of the available colours more slowly. As well as a great learning device, it looks pretty impressive, too.

Chapter 3

Take control: keyboard, mouse, and gamepad

Write some code to get to grips with the keyboard, mouse, and gamepad in Python and Pygame

In the first two chapters, you got to grips with the core concepts of drawing and moving shapes of all types, sizes and colours with Pygame. Now that we know our way around Pygame, we're going to start making things that we can play with that are a bit more interactive. This time, we're going to make two simple programs to learn how to use our keyboard and mouse. The examples in this chapter are a bit longer than in previous chapters, so you may want to download and follow along with the example code from GitHub repository (**rpimag.co/pygamebookgit**).

For our first program, we will use the keyboard; with it, we'll draw a red square and give it some code so it can move left and right and jump, which may conjure memories of a certain heroic plumber. Our second program will use the mouse. Again, we'll create a square which we can pick up, drag around and which, when we let go of our mouse button, will drop to the floor with the help of a little Pygame-programmed gravity. Finally, we'll learn how to modify the keyboard example to support a gamepad. We're focusing on game dynamics at this point, but don't worry: later chapters will explore the more aesthetic aspects of game design!

Pygame keyboard input

On to our first program — **keyboard.py**. Unlike previous chapters, we're not going to chop and change bits of code to show off Pygame's range of capabilities. Instead, we're going to walk through the code to understand what each bit does. Like a lot of things in computing, we are going to start at the top. The first several lines of code should look familiar to you by now; these are the statements we've used previously to import libraries, initialise Pygame, and define our window. The next lines are constants and variables that determine how our keyboard-controlled square should look and where it should be.

```python
import pygame

# Pygame Variables
pygame.init()
clock = pygame.time.Clock()
FPS = 60

WIN_WIDTH = 800
WIN_HEIGHT = 800
surface = pygame.display.set_mode((WIN_WIDTH, WIN_HEIGHT))
pygame.display.set_caption('Pygame Keyboard!')

# Constants
PLAYER_SIZE = 20
MAXJUMP_VY = 25.0
MOVE_SPEED = 1.0
MAX_VX = 10.0

# Variables
player_x = (WIN_WIDTH / 2) - (PLAYER_SIZE / 2)
player_y = WIN_HEIGHT - PLAYER_SIZE
player_vx = 1.0
player_vy = 0.0
gravity = 1.0
```

Following that, we have two functions, **move()** and **quit_game()**, which we'll use to move the square and quit the game. We also have the main loop where we draw all our pixels, including the square, and update the display.

Move()

Before now, almost all the code we've written has been inside our main loop, which becomes a little hard to follow when the code gets long. To make things easier, we've put the code for moving our square into its own function, **move()**, which expects you to supply it with a **direction** and **jump** argument. Let's look at it one chunk at a time.

The first line is a **global** statement. Code inside the **move()** function no longer has the same *scope* as the main loop: although we can *look* at the values of variables defined outside our function, we can't *reassign* their values unless we mark them as **global**. See **rpimag.co/PyScope** for details.

The **move()** function first checks to see whether the player switched direction. In other words, did **move()** receive either of:

- A positive value for **direction** while the player was already moving to the left (is the X velocity, **player_vx**, less than **0**?)
- A negative value for **direction** while the player was already moving to the right (**player_vx > 0**)

If so, we'll stop and change direction. Think about it: if you're running in a straight line, you can't turn right around and keep running at the same speed. You need to stop, turn, and build the speed up again. We do this by setting the X velocity to the base **MOVE_SPEED** (**1.0**) multiplied by the **direction**.

So long as **direction** is not zero, we then add **player_vx** to **player_x**. If **player_vx** is negative, the square moves left; if positive, the square moves right. We don't want our square to run off the screen either; the next few lines stop our square moving if it's at the left or right edge of our window.

```
def move(direction, jump):
    global player_x, player_y, player_vx, player_vy, gravity

    # Did we switch direction along the x axis?
    if (direction > 0 and player_vx < 0) or (direction < 0 and
                                             player_vx > 0):
        player_vx = MOVE_SPEED * direction
```

```python
# Move the player along the x axis
if direction != 0:
    player_x += player_vx

# Keep the player within the screen bounds along the x axis
if player_x > WIN_WIDTH - PLAYER_SIZE:
    player_x = WIN_WIDTH - PLAYER_SIZE
if player_x < 0:
    player_x = 0
```

Next, the code checks to see if **jump** is **True**, and also confirms that the player's square isn't already in the middle of a jump (if the **player_y** coordinate is equal to the window height less the square's height, the square is on the ground). If that's the case, the player's Y velocity (**player_vy**) is set to the maximum. The line **if player_vy > 1.0** checks whether our square is travelling upwards at a speed greater than 1 pixel per frame. If it is, we multiply that value by **0.9** so it will eventually travel less than 1 pixel per second; when that happens, we set the value to **0** so that the square can start falling back to the ground.

Next, our code checks whether our square is in the air: if it is, it will need to come back down (**Figure 3-1**). If the square is in the air, we start adding the **gravity** value to the **player_vy** value; this will make our square move back down. Each time we add **gravity** to the **player_vy** value, we multiply the former by **1.1**; this makes the square speed up as it falls back to the bottom of the screen, just as it would if you threw a ball in the air. The code sets **gravity** to 1.0 when the square lands on the ground.

```python
    # If we're not already jumping, max out the y velocity
    if jump and player_y == WIN_HEIGHT - PLAYER_SIZE:
        player_vy = MAXJUMP_VY

    if player_vy > 1.0:
        # Decrease player_vy throughout the jump
        player_vy = player_vy * 0.9
    else:
        player_vy = 0.0

    # Is our square in the air?
    # Better add some gravity to bring it back down!
```

```
if player_y < WIN_HEIGHT - PLAYER_SIZE:
    player_y += gravity
    gravity = gravity * 1.1
else: # Reset gravity so it starts at 1.0 next time we jump
    gravity = 1.0
```

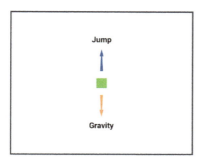

Figure 3-1   Gravity working against the square's Y velocity

Because Pygame Y coordinates decrease towards the top of the window, the code subtracts **player_vy** from **player_y**. We then use the **min()** function to keep the square from falling through the floor: we make sure that the Y coordinate is never greater than **WIN_HEIGHT - PLAYER_SIZE**, which is the square's Y coordinate at the bottom of the window.

The last few lines of code stop the square from moving any faster left or right once our square has jumped in the air. **Figure 3-2** shows the effects of X velocity on your jump distance.

```
# Move the player along the y axis
player_y -= player_vy

# Don't let the player fall through the floor
player_y = min(player_y, WIN_HEIGHT - PLAYER_SIZE)

# Increase x velocity if we're moving but not at maximum.
if direction and abs(player_vx) < MAX_VX:
    # But only if we're not in the air!
    if player_y >= WIN_HEIGHT - PLAYER_SIZE:
        player_vx = player_vx * 1.1
```

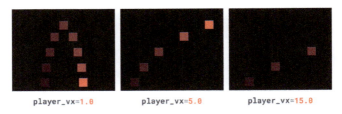

player_vx=1.0   player_vx=5.0   player_vx=15.0

Figure 3-2   The varying effects of the X velocity when jumping

Processing events

The main loop of every Pygame program in this book is one big **while True** loop that keeps on running forever or until we exit the program. Each time our **while** loop runs, we call **pygame.event.get()** to get a list of events that have occurred since the last time the **while** loop ran. This includes system events, like a **QUIT** signal; mouse events, such as a left button click; and keyboard events, like when a button is pressed or released. Once we have the list of events that Pygame received, we iterate over it using a **for** loop and can decide how our program should respond to those events.

> **Quick Tip**
>
> Pygame has a set of handy built-in variables for checking which keys are pressed. We've only used a couple, but you can find the complete list at **rpimag.co/pgkeyvars**

How do we know which key our player pressed? Every Pygame key event has a **key** property that describes which key it represents. If we were to print out the **event.key** property, we would see a lot of numbers, but these aren't the keys that the player pressed. The numbers we would see are *key codes*; they're numbers that are uniquely tied to each key on your keyboard, and programmers can use them to check which keys they represent. For example, the **ESC** key on your keyboard is 27, the **A** key is 97, and **RETURN** is 13. Does this mean that we have to remember a seemingly disconnected bunch of numbers when we're writing keyboard code? Fortunately, the answer is no. Pygame has a ton of constants for checking key codes, which are easier to read and remember when we're writing code.

If the player presses the ESC key (`pygame.K_ESCAPE`), we quit the game. If they press UP ARROW (`pygame.K_UP`), we set the **jump** variable to **True**. The events are arranged in the list in the order that Pygame received them. So, for example, if we wanted to use the keyboard events to type in our player's name, we could trust that we would get all of the letters in the right order and not just a random jumble of characters.

Right after that loop, the code gets a list of pressed keys: if you press LEFT ARROW, it calls the **move()** function with a **direction** of **-1** and the **jump** variable. If you press RIGHT ARROW, it sends a **direction** of **1** instead. And if neither are pressed, it sends a **direction** of **0**. Why two ways of checking for key presses? The answer is somewhat simple: if we had used **pressed_keys** to check whether UP ARROW was pressed, the player would jump repeatedly while you hold that key down. By looking only for the **KEYDOWN** event, you get just one jump per key press. In contrast, you want the player to keep moving while you hold down the RIGHT ARROW or LEFT ARROW keys, and if you look in **pressed_keys** for a key, it will keep returning **True** as long as you hold the key down.

```python
# How to quit our program
def quit_game():
    pygame.quit()
    raise SystemExit

while True:
    surface.fill((0,0,0))

    jump = False

    # Get all events since the last redraw
    for event in pygame.event.get():
        if event.type == pygame.KEYDOWN:
            if event.key == pygame.K_ESCAPE:
                quit_game()
            if event.key == pygame.K_UP:
                jump = True

        if event.type == pygame.QUIT:
            quit_game()
```

```
    pressed_keys = pygame.key.get_pressed()
    if pressed_keys[pygame.K_LEFT]:
        move(-1, jump)
    elif pressed_keys[pygame.K_RIGHT]:
        move(1, jump)
    else:
        move(0, jump)

    pygame.draw.rect(surface, (255,0,0),
                    (player_x, player_y,
                     PLAYER_SIZE, PLAYER_SIZE))
    pygame.display.update()
    clock.tick(FPS)
```

Pygame mouse input

That's enough of the keyboard for now; it's time for the mouse to shine. The mouse is a simple bit of kit, so the code for it is far less complicated than our keyboard code. If you run **mouse.py**, you'll see a familiar red square sitting at the bottom of the screen. Pressing your keyboard keys will do nothing this time, for this square is different. If you want to move it, you've got to use the mouse to pick it up. Drag your mouse over the square, hold down the left mouse button and drag up. Our square moves with our mouse. If you let go of your mouse button, the square will fall back to the bottom of the window. Nice and simple, but how does it work? We start with our usual setup and initialisation followed by constants and variables.

```
import pygame

pygame.init()
clock = pygame.time.Clock()
FPS = 60

WIN_WIDTH = 800
WIN_HEIGHT = 800
window = pygame.display.set_mode((WIN_WIDTH, WIN_HEIGHT))
pygame.display.set_caption('Pygame Mouse!')
```

```
SQUARE_SIZE = 40
square_x = WIN_WIDTH / 2
square_y = WIN_HEIGHT - SQUARE_SIZE
gravity = 2.0
pressed = False
is_dragging = False
```

This time, we have hardly any code at all in our main **for** loop. Most of the work is handled by four functions.

Checking the square

The purpose of **check_bounds()** is to check whether or not our mouse position is within the bounds (edges) of our square (see **Figure 3-3**), and if the left button is pressed, to let other functions know that we're dragging the square. The **is_dragging** global variable indicates whether this is the case. If we were making a fully-fledged game, this function would probably check the position of every game object against the mouse coordinates, but in this example, we're only interested in our red square.

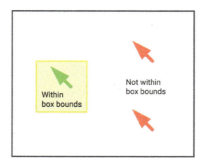

Figure 3-3 Checking the box bounds against the cursor coordinates

If the mouse is currently pressed, the function first defines a rectangle, **box**, that corresponds to the box's current location. Next, it uses **box**'s **collidepoint()** function to determine whether the box overlaps with the result of **pygame.mouse**'s **get_pos()** function. When we call **get_pos()** we get a tuple back with two values: the current X and Y value of the tip of the mouse pointer inside the window. The **collidepoint()** function tells us whether there's a *collision* between the mouse and box. In later chapters, you'll see other ways to determine whether objects on screen are touching each other.

> **Quick Tip**
>
> The X and Y coordinates of a mouse are relative to the left and top of the window, not the computer screen.

Now that we know our mouse is positioned within our square and that we've pressed our mouse button, we can set our `is_dragging` variable to `True` and hide the mouse cursor. Once we stop dragging it, we set `is_dragging` to `False` and show the cursor.

```python
def check_bounds():
    global is_dragging

    if pressed:
        box = pygame.Rect((square_x, square_y,
                           SQUARE_SIZE, SQUARE_SIZE))
        if box.collidepoint(pygame.mouse.get_pos()):
            is_dragging = True
            pygame.mouse.set_visible(0)
    else:
        is_dragging = False
        pygame.mouse.set_visible(1)
```

Once `check_bounds()` has done its job, `check_gravity()` gets to work. Just as we did in **keyboard.py**, `check_gravity()` looks at where our square is in the window: if it's not on the bottom of our window, it will accelerate our square to get there. However, it will only do this if we've let go of our mouse button, because we don't want our shape to fall to the ground when we're holding onto it.

The next function is `draw_square()`: its purpose is easy enough to guess. Based on the adjustments of `check_bounds()` and `check_gravity()`, `draw_square()` will draw the square for us. If our square is being moved around by our mouse, it will draw the square at the mouse coordinates. But if we aren't dragging the square around, it will draw a graceful gravity-driven descent back to the bottom of our window. `draw_square()` has one little trick up its sleeve: as well as affecting the position of our square, it changes its colour: red when not being dragged and green when being dragged. This code could be useful if, instead of a square, we had a character and we wanted to change its graphic to make it look like it was holding onto our cursor. After that, we come to the **quit_game()** function that exits the game.

```python
def check_gravity():
    global gravity, square_y

    # Is our square in the air
    if square_y < WIN_HEIGHT - SQUARE_SIZE:
        if not is_dragging: # have we let go of it?
            square_y += gravity
            gravity = gravity * 1.05
    else:
        square_y = WIN_HEIGHT - SQUARE_SIZE
        gravity = 2.0

def draw_square():
    global square_x, square_y

    if is_dragging:
        square_colour = (0, 255, 0)
        mouse_pos = pygame.mouse.get_pos()
        square_x = mouse_pos[0] - SQUARE_SIZE / 2
        square_y = mouse_pos[1] - SQUARE_SIZE / 2
    else:
        square_colour = (255,0,0)

    pygame.draw.rect(window, square_colour,
                    (square_x, square_y,
                     SQUARE_SIZE, SQUARE_SIZE))

def quit_game():
    pygame.quit()
    raise SystemExit
```

There's not a lot going on in the main loop; we fill the window with a black background, check to see whether the user wants to quit, then find out whether the mouse button has been pressed. After that, we call three functions before updating the screen: **check_bounds()**, **check_gravity()**, and **draw_square()**. Then we update the display and tick the clock.

```python
while True:
    window.fill((0,0,0))

    for event in pygame.event.get():
        if event.type == pygame.KEYDOWN:
            if event.key == pygame.K_ESCAPE:
                quit_game()
        if event.type == pygame.QUIT:
            quit_game()

    pressed = pygame.mouse.get_pressed()[0]

    check_bounds()
    check_gravity()
    draw_square()

    pygame.display.update()
    clock.tick(FPS)
```

The two important things we need to know when using a mouse are where it is and which buttons, if any, have been pressed. Once we know these two things, we can begin to make things happen. In the main loop, we need to determine whether any of the buttons have been pressed; we do this on with **pygame.mouse.get_pressed()**, which returns a tuple of three values: the first is for the left mouse button, the second for the middle mouse button, and the third for the right mouse button. If the button is pressed down, then the value is **True**, otherwise it's **False**. We're not doing anything with the middle or right mouse button, so we can simply check the first value (the left mouse button) with **pygame.mouse.get_pressed()[0]**. If **pygame.mouse.get_pressed()[0]** is **True**, then our player has clicked the button, and we can proceed. In this case we set **pressed** to **True**. We declared it at the top of the program, so we can read its value in any function, and read (and set) its value in the main program. Give the game a try. Can you drop the square and catch it again before it hits the floor?

Pygame gamepad input

It's not difficult at all to add support for gamepad/joystick input. Open **keyboard.py**, and save a copy as **joystick.py**. You'll need to check whether a joystick exists and create a variable to represent it (as well a helper variable). Add the following before your main loop (just before `while True:`):

```python
joystick = None
joy_threshold = 0.05
pygame.joystick.init()
if pygame.joystick.get_count() > 0:
    joystick = pygame.joystick.Joystick(0)
```

Next, replace everything between `jump = False` and the call to `pygame.draw.rect()` with the following. This code will use the joystick if one is detected (otherwise, it uses the keyboard):

```python
    # Get all events since the last redraw
    for event in pygame.event.get():
        if event.type == pygame.KEYDOWN:
            if event.key == pygame.K_ESCAPE:
                quit_game()
            if event.key == pygame.K_UP:
                jump = True

        if event.type == pygame.JOYBUTTONDOWN:
            jump = True

        if event.type == pygame.QUIT:
            quit_game()

    if joystick:
        x_axis = joystick.get_axis(0)
        if abs(x_axis) <= joy_threshold:
            move(0,jump)
        elif x_axis > joy_threshold:
            move(1, jump)
        elif x_axis <= -joy_threshold:
            move(-1, jump)
```

```python
        else:
            pressed_keys = pygame.key.get_pressed()
            if pressed_keys[pygame.K_LEFT]:
                move(-1, jump)
            elif pressed_keys[pygame.K_RIGHT]:
                move(1, jump)
            else:
                move(0, jump)
```

The joystick **get_axis()** function lets you read the position of an analogue joystick axis. It returns a value of approximately zero when nothing is pressed (in other words, when the joystick is centred), a value between zero and 1 for one direction, and between negative 1 and zero for the other. Axis 0 represents the X axis; you can use **joystick.get_axis(1)** for the Y axis. If you find that your square is moving even when you're not pressing the joystick, try increasing the value of **joy_threshold** to **0.10** or higher.

What you've learned

You've learned that Pygame creates a list of events that occurred every time the frame is updated, and that you can work through them to check for events that you want to use. You also learned that you can get a list of all the currently pressed keys without needing to poll for events. You learned that Pygame receives key codes when buttons are pressed, but has a big list of key code events that you can use so you don't have to remember all of the numbers. You learned that you can get mouse events whenever you like, and that you can get coordinates of where the mouse is and which buttons are pressed. You've also learned how to simulate gravity and jumping, and you've thought about how things move in the real world too. Congratulations! You now have the beginnings of a real game.

Chapter 4

Your first game

Now that we've covered making shapes, animating them, and setting up control mechanisms, we have everything we need to make our first proper game

We're going to make an old-school drop-down game where platforms rise up from the floor and try to crush our player against the roof; the only way to survive is by dropping through the gaps in the platforms. Unlike our previous examples, we're not going to write a program that just runs: we will also make a simple start screen and a game over screen. We still have a few things we're going to learn about along the way, like loading images and displaying them, but the biggest is the introduction of *sprites* and *collision masks*.

A sprite is a two-dimensional bitmap similar to the shapes you've seen in previous chapters. Traditionally, the term sprite referred to shapes that were drawn by specialised graphics hardware. Early computers and video game systems lacked the computational power to let programmers write code that drew both the playfield and shapes on screen every time the screen refreshed (as we did in previous chapters). Instead, these systems would let you define areas of memory that contained a bitmapped representation of the shapes you needed (your sprites), and you'd tell the computer's graphic chip where you wanted it to put that shape. The specialised graphics hardware made short work of that task, freeing up the limited CPUs of the time for other tasks.

Modern computers are fast enough to let you do everything manually, but you can make your code a lot simpler if you take advantage of Pygame's built-in support for sprites. It makes it simple to move a sprite from place to place, and Pygame also has built-in functions that make it easy to figure out if one sprite has collided with another. As you'll soon see, much of the logic involved in video games centres around collision detection and what to do when one sprite bumps into another!

How does the game work?

Before we write any code, it's important to have a solid understanding of how our game is going to work. When the game starts, our avatar (a red rectangle) will drop down from the top of the screen. Every two seconds, a white platform will start to rise from the bottom of the screen; if our character lands on one of these platforms, it will start to rise along with it. If we go off the top of the game screen, it's game over. Defeat is not assured, however: we can move our character with the left and right arrow keys so it can drop down through the randomly positioned gaps in the platforms. The aim of the game is to stay alive as long as possible. It sounds easy, but things get tougher as time goes on, because the platforms will move faster over time.

What is a class?

Before we can get into sprites, let's talk about data structures and classes. Python gives us many ways to represent data, such as variables, lists, tuples, and dictionaries. Each data type exists to help us organise and store data in a way that makes it easy for us to reuse and reference throughout our games. A class is another such structure that helps us to organise our code and objects. Classes are designed to be a kind of blueprint for bits of code that might need to be reused again and again. Before we get into classes, let's look at dictionaries and lists.

In previous chapters, we've almost always used variables that have one value, but there are other variables that can contain multiple values — like tuples, for example, which are similar to lists but differ in important ways (for example, you can't append to a tuple).

Data structures that can contain more than one item are very useful as we start to make bigger and more powerful programs. When we write small programs, having variables with a single value is great, because we can see which variables are doing what. However, as programs grow, it can get harder to name variables in a way that relates to what we're trying to do. Imagine a game where there's more than one player, like an MMO (Massively Multiplayer Online game); if we wrote code like we've done before, we'd need multiple sets of variables for each player. It doesn't take a genius to realise the code is going to get unmanageably long, very quickly.

What if we wanted to handle four or 100 or 1,000 players at the same time? Do we hand-write variables for every single one? No. We can use lists and dictionaries instead. Lists are pretty simple; you can initialise them by supplying a comma-separated sequence of values in square brackets:

```python
item_list = [1, 2, 4, 8, 16]
```

You can refer to an item in a list by putting its index in square brackets after the list name (list indexes start counting at 0):

```python
print(item_list[0])
```

You can add an item to a list:

```python
item_list.append(32)
```

You can remove items from lists, too:

```python
item_list.remove(16)
```

A dictionary is a data structure with multiple keys that have values. You can think of a dictionary as you would its real-world counterpart: if you want to know what something is, you search through until you find the definition. Here's a dictionary that represents a rectangle:

```python
a_rectangle = { "x" : 5,
                "y" : 10,
                "width" : 20,
                "height" : 30
              }
```

So, let's say we want to know the value of **x** in the **a_rectangle** dictionary; all we have to do is request **a_rectangle["x"]**. We can do the same with any other value that is stored in it, and we can also save or change values.

If the value **a_rectangle["y"]** is 10 and we wanted to change it to 25, we'd enter **a_rectangle["y"] = 25**, just like setting any other variable. Dictionaries are useful, because they let us group values together in a way that's easy to read and easy to access with code. If we revisit our MMO game thought exercise, we'd quickly realise that we'd still need 100 variables to handle 100 players, even though we've made things tidier and more usable.

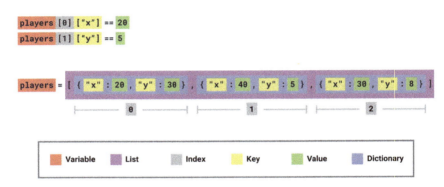

Figure 4-1   A breakdown of the various components of a dictionary

Figure 4-1 shows a list of players that contains three dictionaries. Each dictionary contains the **x** and **y** positions of a different player. **Figure 4-2** shows how you'd call the **append()** function to add a new player dictionary to that list.

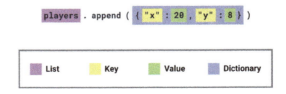

Figure 4-2   Here's a handy reference to help with appending a dictionary item to a list

Our `a_rectangle` dictionary from earlier would certainly do the job of representing a rectangle; we have everything we need to make a rectangle: `width`, `height`, `x`, and `y`. It's great, but what if we want to make another rectangle with different characteristics? We could simply write it again:

```python
rectangle_one = { "x" : 20,
                  "y" : 15,
                  "width" : 30,
                  "height" : 50
                }
rectangle_two = { "x" : 10,
                  "y" : 35,
                  "width" : 40,
                  "height" : 70
                }
```

But that's a little messy. Instead, we could create a function to make rectangles for us:

```python
def rectangle_maker(x, y, width, height):
    return { "x" : x,
             "y" : y,
             "width" : width,
             "height" : height
           }
rectangle_one = rectangle_maker(20, 15, 30, 50)
rectangle_two = rectangle_maker(10, 35, 40, 70)
```

That's better, but to make rectangles a more convenient thing to create quickly, we've had to write a function which builds one and passes the new 'rectangle' (it's not really a rectangle, it's a dictionary describing something that *could* be a rectangle) back to whatever bit of code wanted it. This does the job, but it's not very semantically rich.

Classes do all that we just looked at and more: they can keep track of themselves and their properties; they can contain functions that can execute code that affects the properties in a clever way, rather than having to trigger things manually. Classes can also be *extended*; that is, a class can take all the properties and abilities of another class and add new properties and abilities to it. If we were to make a class to represent squares, we would first make a class to represent what a rectangle is:

```python
class Rectangle():
    def __init__(self, x, y, width, height):
        self.x = x
        self.y = y
        self.width = width
        self.height = height
```

Our class **Rectangle** has a function, **__init__()**. This is a special function; when we want to create a new rectangle, we simply call **Rectangle** and pass it the values we want to use into it, where we initialise four properties — **x**, **y**, **width**, and **height** — similar to dictionaries, but with all the power that classes provide.

```python
rectangle_one = Rectangle(20, 15, 30, 50)
rectangle_two = Rectangle(10, 35, 40, 70)
```

When we call **Rectangle** like this, we are triggering something called *instantiation*. In its simplest terms, instantiation means we're creating something new (an *instance*) from a blueprint (our class) that can operate independently from other objects in our code. When we instantiate a new **Rectangle**, that special function **__init__()** will be called and will receive the variables we pass through to it.

There's something a little different here, though: our **__init__()** function is expecting five arguments to be passed to it, but we only passed four, and Python didn't complain. Why is this? When we instantiate a new **Rectangle**, **self** gets passed through to the **__init__()** function by the class itself and it refers to its 'self'. With **self**, we can create as many **Rectangles** as we like and have functions inside of the class operate only on a given instance of the class, assign values that belong to the class, and run code that only affects itself. It's this useful characteristic that makes classes far more useful than standard dictionaries. We can also reference the properties and functions of each instance of our **Rectangles** using '**.**' instead of having to use **[ ]**.

If we wanted to give the Rectangle a function (known as a *method* when used in the context of classes) to calculate its area, we could do so easily:

```python
def area(self):
    return self.width * self.height
```

And we could call that method just as easily:

```python
print(rectangle_one.area()) # displays 1500
print(rectangle_two.area()) # displays 2800
```

Variables and prerequisites

The first part of our code contains the `import` statements and variables we're going to need to get our game off the ground. By now, much of this should look pretty familiar. We're also loading images that we'll be using for our start and game over screens. We could draw the graphical user interface (GUI) with code, but by using images we're saving ourselves time and effort at the cost of just a few kilobytes.

Here is the usual initialisation, along with the constants and variables that we'll use to control how the game window looks.

```python
import pygame
import random

pygame.init()
clock = pygame.time.Clock()
FPS = 60

title_image = pygame.image.load("assets/title.jpg")
game_over_image = pygame.image.load("assets/game_over.jpg")

WIN_WIDTH = 400
WIN_HEIGHT = 600
window = pygame.display.set_mode((WIN_WIDTH, WIN_HEIGHT))
pygame.display.set_caption('Drop!')
```

The player

On screen, our avatar isn't a complicated construct: at its simplest, it's a red rectangle. However, rather than define our own **Rectangle** class from scratch, we're going to use a class that's part of Pygame: **Sprite**. It offers Pygame's implementation of sprites, which simplifies drawing your objects, combining them into groups, and detecting collisions between them.

Our code will extend the **Sprite** class into our custom **Player** class. We indicate that **Player** inherits from its parent class by enclosing the parent class name (**pygame.sprite.Sprite**) in parentheses after the name of the class. Here's the full definition of the **Player** class:

```python
class Player(pygame.sprite.Sprite):
    def __init__(self):
        super().__init__()

        self.gravity = 1
        self.x = WIN_WIDTH / 2
        self.y = 1
        self.speed_x = 3
        self.direction = 0

        self.image = pygame.Surface((10, 25))
        self.image.fill((255, 0, 0))

        # Create a collision mask
        self.mask = pygame.mask.from_surface(self.image)

        # Get the image's rectangle and place it at x, y
        self.rect = self.image.get_rect()
        self.rect.midbottom = (self.x, self.y)

    def set_direction(self, direction=0):
        self.direction = direction

    def update(self):
        self.x = self.x + direction * self.speed_x
        self.y = self.y + self.gravity
```

```
        if self.x > WIN_WIDTH:
            self.x = 0
        if self.x < 0:
            self.x = WIN_WIDTH

        self.rect.midbottom = (self.x, self.y)

    def check_collisions(self, all_sprites):
        # Check for collisions with all platforms
        platforms = [p for p in all_sprites
                     if isinstance(p, Platform)]
        hits = pygame.sprite.spritecollide(self, platforms,
                False, collided=pygame.sprite.collide_mask)
        if hits:
            self.gravity = 0
            self.y = hits[0].rect.top + 1
        elif self.y >= WIN_HEIGHT:
            self.gravity = 0
            self.y = WIN_HEIGHT + 1
        else:
            self.gravity = 2
```

Inside the **__init__()** method, we first call the **__init__()** method from the parent class. Next, we set several properties of the player: the amount of gravity, the **x** and **y** position, the speed at which the player moves along the x axis, and its current direction of movement. After that, we define an image to represent the rectangular player, fill it with red, and then create a *collision mask*, which defines the boundaries used for detecting collisions. In the case of the player, it's the same shape as its image. Finally, we set a **rect** property to represent the player's rectangle, which we can use to set the player's position on screen. We place its middle bottom at the **x** and **y** position.

The next method, **set_direction()**, takes an argument of 0, -1, or 1, and is used to represent the direction you moved the player in. That's followed by the **update()** method, which modifies the **x** and **y** properties: we multiply the direction by the X speed and add that to **x**. Next, we add the current value of gravity to **y**. If we exceed the width of the window, we set **x** to 0, and vice-versa. This wraps your player around to the opposite side of the screen, which we can sometimes use as a shortcut to reach a gap.

Before we look at the next method, let's talk about the core gameplay (**Figure 4-3**): we want our player to fall when there is either a gap in the platform or no platform at all. We also want the player to travel up with the platform if there is no gap present. To code this logic, we could check the position of all of the platforms every frame and write some code that would figure out whether or not our avatar is on top of a platform, but that wouldn't be at all efficient. Instead, we're doing something simpler: use Pygame's built-in collision detection to tell us whether the collision masks of our player and platforms are touching one another.

Figure 4-3   The 'Drop' game challenges you to fall and navigate through a sequence of platforms

We finish the definition of the `Player` class with a `check_collisions()` method. This method calls `pygame.sprite.spritecollide()` to check whether the player's collision mask has overlapped with any of the platforms' collision mask. If so, it sets gravity to 0 and moves the player to be 1 pixel inside the bounds of the platform it collided with (represented as the first element in the hits array, **hits[0]**). The reason for this extra pixel is to keep the player steady as long as it is atop a platform. Otherwise, in the next frame, **gravity** would be set to 1, and the player would resume falling in the frame that follows that. This would give a slight hopping movement to the player, which doesn't look very nice.

If there hasn't been a collision with one of the platforms, we check to see if the player has landed on the 'floor' (if **y** is greater than or equal to the window height). If so, we do the same thing we did with the platforms, keeping the player anchored at 1 pixel past the window height. If there were no collisions with anything, **gravity** gets restored to 1, and the player starts falling again.

The platforms

Like our player, the platforms are nothing fancy: white rectangles which are the width of the screen, each with a gap that the character can drop through to the next platform. Here's the definition of the **Platform** class:

```python
class Platform(pygame.sprite.Sprite):
    HEIGHT = 20
    GAP = 50
    def __init__(self):
        super().__init__()

        self.x = WIN_WIDTH / 2
        self.y = WIN_HEIGHT
        self.speed = 2

        self.image = pygame.Surface((WIN_WIDTH, self.HEIGHT),
                                    pygame.SRCALPHA)
        self.image.fill((255, 255, 255, 255))  # solid platform

        # Draw a gap
        gap_loc = random.randint(0, WIN_WIDTH-self.GAP)
        pygame.draw.rect(self.image, (255,255,255,0),
                         (gap_loc, 0, self.GAP, self.HEIGHT))
```

```python
        # Create a collision mask
        self.mask = pygame.mask.from_surface(self.image)
        # Scaling to ignore collisions halfway through the gap
        self.mask = self.mask.scale((WIN_WIDTH,
                                    self.HEIGHT * .5))

        self.rect = self.image.get_rect()
        self.rect.center = (self.x, self.y)

    def update(self):
        self.y = self.y - self.speed
        self.rect.center = (self.x, self.y)
        # Destroy platforms when they move offscreen
        if self.rect.bottomleft[1] <= 0:
            self.kill()
```

As with the **Player** class, the **Platform** class extends the **Sprite** class. Before its **__init__()** method, we set a class constant for the platform height (**HEIGHT**) and the width of the platform gaps (**GAP**). In its **__init__()** method, we call the **__init__()** method from the parent class. Then, we set the **x**, **y**, and **speed** properties of the platform. Just as we did with the player, we create a **Surface** object and assign it to the platform's **image** property. However, we use the **pygame.SRCALPHA** option to tell it to use alpha blending. This is because the platforms are irregularly shaped (unlike the player, platforms have gaps). We first fill the platform image with white (RGB values of 255, 255, 255), with an alpha channel value of 255, which makes it opaque. Next, we calculate a random gap location, and draw a gap, again white, but with an alpha of 0, which makes it completely transparent.

After that, we set the collision mask, but we scale it to half its height. This is to prevent a collision from occurring when the player is more than halfway through the gap; otherwise, the player would 'hop' to the top of the platform when part-way through, which would seem to defy physics. Finally, we set a **rect** property to represent the platform's rectangle, which we then use to set its position on screen.

The **update()** method is relatively simple. It subtracts **speed** from the **y** position, thus moving it up, and sets the centre of the platform to **x**, **y**.

However, if a platform has moved off the screen, it destroys it by calling its `kill()` method. That way, we're not spending any CPU cycles on platforms that are off screen.

Starting and stopping the game

Now that the two classes are defined, we can get on to the main program. There are only three functions within the program itself:

```python
def restart_game():
    global all_sprites, player, platform_delay, game_started
    all_sprites.empty()
    player = Player()
    all_sprites.add(player)
    platform_delay = 2000
    pygame.time.set_timer(NEW_PLATFORM, platform_delay)
    game_started = True

def check_game_over():
    global game_ended, game_started
    if player.rect.bottomleft[1] <= 0:
        game_ended = True
        game_started = False
```

The `restart_game()` function initialises four global variables to their start-of-game defaults and also starts a timer that will be fired every 2000 milliseconds (two seconds) to add a new platform. We'll see how that works when we get to the main game loop.

The `all_sprites` variable is a sprite group, and when we call a method on the group, the method gets triggered on every member of the group. We can add to the group, and when we call the `kill()` method of a `Platform` object, it gets removed from the group.

The `check_game_over()` function checks to see whether the player has gone off the top of the screen. If so, it sets the `game_ended` variable to `True` and `game_started` to `False`. As with the examples in the last chapter, `quit_game()` takes care of shutting down the game when you're done.

The main game loop

Now we come to the heart of the game. Before we begin the main loop, we initialise some game-specific variables related to the state of the game. The `NEW_PLATFORM` variable represents a user-defined event that is triggered every time the timer we set up in `restart_game()` is triggered. You're allowed to define any number of events between the value of `pygame.USEREVENT` and `pygame.NUMEVENTS - 1`. Although the zero doesn't accomplish anything, we express the value as `USEREVENT + 0` to remind us that we should use a different offset (`+ 1`, `+ 2`, etc.) if we add any other events to our game.

```python
all_sprites = pygame.sprite.Group()
player = None
platform_delay = 2000
game_started = False
game_ended = False
NEW_PLATFORM = pygame.USEREVENT + 0
while True:
    for event in pygame.event.get():
        if event.type == pygame.KEYDOWN:
            if event.key == pygame.K_ESCAPE:
                quit_game()
        if event.type == pygame.QUIT:
            quit_game()
        if event.type == NEW_PLATFORM:
            new_platform = Platform()
            all_sprites.add(new_platform)
            platform_delay = max(800, platform_delay - 50)
            pygame.time.set_timer(NEW_PLATFORM, platform_delay)

    window.fill((0, 0, 0))

    # Handle keyboard input
    direction = 0
    pressed_keys = pygame.key.get_pressed()
    if pressed_keys[pygame.K_LEFT]:
        direction = -1
    elif pressed_keys[pygame.K_RIGHT]:
        direction = 1
```

```
    elif pressed_keys[pygame.K_SPACE]:
        if not game_started:
            restart_game()

    if game_started: # Move, check collisions, and draw sprites
        player.set_direction(direction)
        all_sprites.update()

        player.check_collisions(all_sprites)
        check_game_over()

        all_sprites.draw(window)
    elif game_ended:
        window.blit(game_over_image, (0, 150))

    else:
        window.blit(title_image, (0, 150))

    pygame.display.update()
    clock.tick(FPS)
```

The main loop runs once for each frame of the game. The first thing we do in the main loop is to check for events. If the user quit the program, for example, by closing the window, we exit the game. If we received a **NEW_PLATFORM** event, we add a new platform, decrease the delay, but we use the **max()** function to ensure we don't go below 800 milliseconds, or just under a second. After that, we reset the timer with the new delay.

Next, we use **window.fill()** to fill the screen with a black background, then we check to see which key was pressed. If the player pressed left, we'll set direction to **-1**; if right, **1**. If neither was pressed, we leave it at zero. The last key we check for is the **SPACE** key — if the game hasn't started yet, pressing the **SPACE** key starts it.

The next step of the loop is to check whether the game started. If it has, we first set the direction of the player, and then we call the **update()** method of the **all_sprites** group, which calls the **update()** method of each **Sprite** in the group. We then check for collisions, check whether the game should be over, and use **`all_sprites`**'s **`draw()`** method to draw the objects on screen.

If the game hasn't started, we check to see if the game has ended. If it has, we use **`blit()`** to show the game over image (**Figure 4-4**), which we loaded at the top of the program. If the game has neither started nor ended, we show the title image (which we also loaded earlier, and is shown in **Figure 4-5**). After that, we update the display and trigger another tick of the game clock!

Figure 4-4 Just like our start screen, our game over screen is simply an image drawn straight onto our surface when we need it

BLITTING

Blitting is essentially a fancy way of saying 'pasting.' When we blit something, we take the pixels of our surface and then we change the pixels so that they're the same as the image we're adding. This means that anything that was beneath the area being blitted is lost. It's a lot like cutting letters out of a newspaper and supergluing them onto a piece of paper: whatever was beneath the newspaper clipping is gone forever, but we can see what we cut out of the newspaper just fine.

And that's it! Using all the skills we've already acquired (and a few new ones), we've built our first fully-fledged game. Like all good games, we've got a start, a middle, and an end.

Figure 4-5 We could code our title screen, but using an image is simpler

Run the game and give it a try! You'll find it starts out easy, but once the platforms start appearing faster and faster, it gets tough. Remember that your player can scroll off the edge of the screen and reappear on the other side. Sometimes the shortest path to a gap in a platform is off the edge of the screen!

Chapter 5

Pygame Soundboard

Learn about loading and playing sounds in your Pygame projects by making a fun farmyard soundboard

In the previous chapter, we put together a simple video game in which we tried to avoid the dreadful fate of being crushed by a ceiling by dropping through platforms into the space below. It didn't have the fanciest graphics, but, then again, fancy graphics aren't everything. One simple thing that can enhance our players' experience is adding sounds. We're going to learn how sounds work with Pygame by putting together a soundboard with some simple controls. We'll learn about loading sounds, playing them, adjusting the sound controls, and using the mixer to stop everything. We'll also put together some code to create the soundboard buttons; this will draw on our knowledge of lists, dictionaries, and mouse events from previous chapters.

While MP3 is a popular format for playing music and sounds, the downside is that it's a proprietary technology whose patents only expired within the last decade. Although MP3 support in Pygame and other free and open-source libraries has improved since, we are going to use OGG, an open sound format that Pygame supports. All the sounds for this project are available on GitHub (**rpimag.co/pygamebookgit**), in OGG and MP3 format.

First things first

Just like any Pygame project, there are a couple of things we need to sort out before we can get our hands dirty writing some real code. The first dozen lines should be familiar to you by now: first we have our **import** statements, our usual initialisation, then we set the properties of our window:

```python
import pygame
from pygame import image, mixer, Vector2
import itertools

pygame.init()
FPS = 60
WIN_WIDTH = 600
WIN_HEIGHT = 650
clock = pygame.time.Clock()
window = pygame.display.set_mode((WIN_WIDTH, WIN_HEIGHT))
pygame.display.set_caption("Soundboard")
```

We first define several constants that we'll use throughout the program, followed by the **buttons** array; when we're ready to create our buttons, we'll append some dictionaries to this to keep track of all of the soundboard buttons. On the next line, we have our **stop_btn** dictionary; when we create our stop button, it'll behave much like the rest of the buttons except that it will stop all current sounds playing. Since it's unique, our stop button gets its own variable.

After the stop button is defined, you'll see the variables used for making the buttons flash as you click them: **flashed** indicates whether the button is flashed, **CLEAR_FLASH** is a user-defined event that we'll use to turn the flash off. You can define multiple user events, but if you created another, you'd define it as **pygame.USEREVENT + 1** (**+ 2** for the next one, and so forth on up to the value of **pygame.NUMEVENTS - 1**). **FLASH_TIMER**, defined along with other constants, determines how long the button is highlighted. You'll see how this gets used later in the program. Finally, this section has a variable for the volume, and a **Rect** to represent the volume slider:

```python
DEFAULT_VOLUME = 0.2
IMAGES_PATH = "assets/images"
SOUNDS_PATH = "assets/sounds"
```

```
FLASH_TIMER = 250
FLASH_COLOUR = (255, 255, 255, 128)
ANIMALS = ["sheep", "rooster", "pig", "mouse",
           "horse", "dog", "cow", "chicken", "cat"]

buttons = []
stop_btn = {"image": image.load(f"{IMAGES_PATH}/stop.png"),
            "pos": (275, 585)}
flashed = None
CLEAR_FLASH = pygame.USEREVENT + 0

volume = DEFAULT_VOLUME
volume_slider_rect = pygame.Rect(450, 610, 100, 5)
```

At the very end of the program (shown later in this chapter), we have our familiar old main loop. It's looking a lot smaller than the last chapter: that's because we've broken out all the main loop code into separate functions. Just as before, our main loop is responsible for wiping the screen; handling mouse, keyboard, and system events; and calling functions to draw in our window. Let's go back to the top of the program now and have a look at how we get the Pygame mixer to make some sounds.

Mix it up with Pygame mixer

To make sounds in Pygame, you'll need to use Pygame's built-in *mixer*. The mixer is similar to a real-world audio mixer board (see **Figure 5-1**): all game sounds pass through it. When a sound is in the mixer, it can be adjusted in a variety of ways, volume being one. When our mixer is finished, it passes the sound through to an output — our speakers. Before we start loading or playing any sounds, we need to initialise the mixer, just as we need to initialise Pygame before we draw things.

Our first sound

You can play sounds a couple of different ways in Pygame: you can either play a stream of sound, in which the sound is played as it's loaded, or you can create and play a sound object, which loads the sound, stores it in memory, and then plays it. Each way of playing sound is good

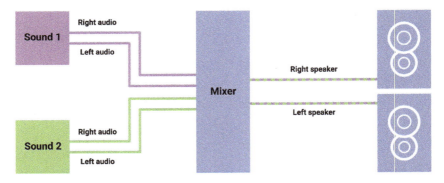

Figure 5-1 How the Pygame audio mixer works

for different instances. Streaming is better, for example, when we want to create background music that plays while we are doing other things, whereas the sound object is a better choice for when we want to play short sounds quickly and often.

The sound object fits the bill for our soundboard better than the sound stream, so we'll use those for our buttons a little later on. First, we're going to add some ambience to our soundboard with a little background audio from a farm. Background audio usually loops without any sort of user interaction, and streaming audio can be set to loop without too much trouble, so that's what we're going to do. Before we can play any music, we need to load it: on the next line we tell Pygame to load our background audio, **farm.ogg**. This loads the audio into our mixer, but it won't play straight away. On the next line, we call **pygame.mixer.music.play(-1)**, which starts playing our sound file:

```
pygame.mixer.init()
pygame.mixer.music.load(f"{SOUNDS_PATH}/OGG/farm.ogg")
pygame.mixer.music.play(-1)
```

The number we pass is the number of times we want our sound to repeat before it stops playing. We've passed **-1**, which means that it will loop forever, or until we stop it. If we ran our soundboard at this point, we'd have a lovely big blank window with some calming farm sounds playing, but that's a bit bare. It's time to make some buttons!

Here a button, there a button, EVERYWHERE a button!

So, how are we going to make these buttons? We could do what we've done in previous chapters and draw some shapes and add text to them; that would certainly do the job, but it won't look great. Instead, we're going to make our buttons out of images your expert has put together for each animal sound. If you want to peek at the buttons before loading them, they're in the folder `code/ch05/assets/images`, which you can grab from the GitHub repo.

Each button has a silhouette of an animal. It will make the sound this animal makes when we click it, but how do we make an image make a sound? We are going to be using lists and dictionaries again: remember the `buttons` variable from the program initialisation? It starts out empty, but now it's time to add some dictionaries describing our buttons to it. We iterate over the list of animal names (`ANIMALS`) with a loop. Each time through, the next animal is assigned to the variable `animal`. We also want to lay the buttons out in a 3×3 grid, so we've created an iterator named `coords` using the `itertools.product()` function (we'll have more to say on this in "Python's iterators" on page 70).

Finally, we load the image and sound for each animal and create a new dictionary for each animal that we append to the `buttons` array. Each dictionary has three keys (or properties: the terms are interchangeable). The first one is `image`, which contains the image for that button. In previous dictionaries, we've stored strings in dictionaries and then used those strings to load images when we've needed them; this time, however, we load each image with `pygame.image.load()` and store it in the dictionary. This saves time when we need to draw something many times, and seeing as the image never changes, it makes sense to have it there. Our next key is `pos`; this is a Pygame class instance (`Vector2`) that contains the X and Y coordinates for where our buttons will be drawn. The last property, `sound`, is similar to our `image` property, except it contains a sound.

```
# Create animal sound buttons
coords = itertools.product([0, 1, 2], repeat=2)
offset = Vector2(25, 25)
for animal in ANIMALS:
```

```
position = Vector2(next(coords)) * 200 + offset
img = image.load(f"{IMAGES_PATH}/{animal}.png")
snd = mixer.Sound(f"{SOUNDS_PATH}/OGG/{animal}.ogg")
buttons.append({"image": img,
                "pos": position,
                "sound": snd})
```

We loaded each sound as an object, which means that they're essentially self-contained in terms of how they work. With the background audio we loaded earlier, we passed the data straight through into the mixer and played it through the latter. A sound object, however, has functions that let us control the audio by itself. For example, we could call **sound.play()** and the sound would play, or we could call **sound.stop()**, but it would only apply to the sound we were calling those functions on: if we had two sounds playing at the same time and we stopped only one, the other would keep playing.

Python's iterators

An iterator is a Python data structure that can be used in a loop, but because we already have a loop (**for animal in ANIMALS**), we'll call the **next()** function on the iterator (**coords**) each time we want to fetch a value.

The **product()** function takes a list as an argument, and when given the **repeat=2** argument, it creates a sequence of all *ordered pairs* of 0, 1, and 2: **(0,0)**, **(0,1)**, **(0,2)**, and so forth. As the name implies, order is significant for ordered pairs, which means that (0,1) and (1,0) are considered different pairs. This is useful for us because the pairs describe a 3×3 grid nicely:

```
(0,0)  (0,1)  (0,2)
(1,0)  (1,1)  (1,2)
(2,0)  (2,1)  (2,2)
```

But, if we placed all the buttons in such a tight grid, they'd overlap, and it would be quite a mess. Instead, we want pairs like this:

```
( 25,  25)  ( 25, 225)  ( 25, 425)
(225,  25)  (225, 225)  (225, 425)
(425,  25)  (425, 225)  (425, 425)
```

We solve this by multiplying each coordinate by 200 (0, 1, and 2 become 0, 200, and 400) and adding an offset of 25 to each (25, 200, 425). We're using Pygame's two-dimensional **Vector2** class to facilitate this: if we multiply a **Vector2** by an integer, each number in the pair gets multiplied by that number. We can't add an integer to a vector, so we represent the offset as another **Vector2** of (25, 25).

Drawing our buttons

If we were to run our program now, we would still only see a blank white window. We still haven't drawn the buttons yet — we've only loaded the necessary data to make them work. In our main loop at the end of the program, we will call the function **draw_buttons()**. You may be surprised that we can use such a small amount of code to draw nine buttons. Because we did the hard work of loading our images and sounds earlier, we have very little to do when we draw the buttons to our window. We have a **for** loop which works through the **buttons** list; for every dictionary it finds in the list, it will draw a button onto our window. A button must flash for the first 250 milliseconds (defined earlier in **FLASH_TIMER**) after it's been clicked. Later, you'll see some code that sets the **flashed** variable to the button that was clicked; the **flashed** variable will be cleared automatically after **FLASH_TIMER** has elapsed. But if the variable **flashed** refers to the current button we're drawing, we'll call the **create_flashed_button()** function to make it appear highlighted:

```python
def draw_buttons():
    for button in buttons + [stop_btn]:
        img = button["image"]
        if flashed == img:
            img = create_flashed_button(img)
        window.blit(img, button["pos"])

def create_flashed_button(img):
    flashed = pygame.Surface(img.get_rect().size,
                             pygame.SRCALPHA)
    flashed.blit(img, (0, 0))
    flashed.fill(FLASH_COLOUR, None, pygame.BLEND_RGBA_MULT)
    return flashed
```

The **create_flashed_button()** function creates a surface the same size as the button image but enables the alpha (transparency) channel. We then **blit()** the image into that surface, and fill it with white (255, 255, 255) but with a roughly 50% (128/255) alpha channel, which creates the desired effect. That white colour with an alpha channel was defined earlier as the constant **FLASH_COLOUR**.

Clicking buttons

Now that we have a soundboard with buttons, we need to make those buttons do something. The **handle_button_click()** function is called when the user clicks the mouse. Because we'll be modifying the value of **flashed**, we declare it as **global**. We iterate through the **button** list, and for each button, get a **rect** that corresponds to that button. We define the **rect**'s top left as the button's position. We then check to see if the mouse pointer and that **rect** collide (see **Figure 5-2**). If so, we know the button was clicked. We set the **flashed** variable to that same button and set a timer that will raise a user-defined event in 250 milliseconds (the value of **FLASH_TIMER**). We'll watch for that event in the main loop later and clear the flash. Finally, we set the sound's volume and play it. At this point, we can return from the function: the user can click only one button at a time, so there's no point in checking the others.

After that loop, we do something similar for the stop button. However, instead of playing a sound, we tell the mixer to stop playing.

```python
def handle_button_click():
    global flashed
    mouse_pos = pygame.mouse.get_pos()

    for button in buttons:
        rect = button["image"].get_rect(topleft=button["pos"])
        if rect.collidepoint(mouse_pos):
            flashed = button["image"]
            pygame.time.set_timer(CLEAR_FLASH, FLASH_TIMER)
            button["sound"].set_volume(volume)
            button["sound"].play()
            return
```

```
# Check stop button
rect = stop_btn["image"].get_rect(topleft=stop_btn["pos"])
if rect.collidepoint(mouse_pos):
    flashed = stop_btn["image"]
    pygame.time.set_timer(CLEAR_FLASH, FLASH_TIMER)
    mixer.stop()
```

Figure 5-2 The imaginary bounding box that surrounds the buttons

IT'S LOUD! Oh... it's quiet now...

So, we've loaded sounds, played them, and stopped them dead, but what if we just wanted to make the sounds a little quieter? This is simple enough to achieve. Each of our sound objects has a **set_volume()** function which can be passed a value between 0.0 and 1.0. 0.0 is silent, while 1.0 is full volume. If you pass a value larger than 1.0, it will become 1.0, and if you pass a value less than 0.0, it will become 0.0. To begin, we need to make a volume slider. In the **draw_volume_slider()** function, we draw two rectangles. The first rectangle represents the range of 0.0 to 1.0, and the second rectangle is an indicator of the current volume. When we first start our soundboard, the volume is set at 0.2, so our indicator should appear towards the left of the slider.

Just before we call **draw_volume_slider()** in our main loop, we call **update_volume()**, where we look at the mouse position and whether its left button is pressed. If it is, our user is likely trying to set the volume level. We work out where the mouse is on a scale between 0.0 and 1.0 on our indicator (see **Figure 5-3**) and set the volume to the new level. Then, when our **draw_volume_slider()** function is called, the indicator will be drawn at the correct position. Now, when we next click a sound, and call the **set_volume()** function on the corresponding sound object, the volume will be at our chosen level.

```python
def draw_volume_slider():
    # Draw slider background
    pygame.draw.rect(window, (229, 229, 229),
                     volume_slider_rect)

    # Draw slider handle
    volume_pos = volume * 100
    handle_rect = pygame.Rect(450 + volume_pos, 600, 10, 25)
    pygame.draw.rect(window, (204, 204, 204), handle_rect)

def update_volume():
    global volume

    if pygame.mouse.get_pressed()[0]:
        mouse_pos = pygame.mouse.get_pos()
        if volume_slider_rect.collidepoint(mouse_pos):
            volume = float((mouse_pos[0] - 450)) / 100
```

Now we're just about at the end of the program. That just leaves a function to quit the game and our relatively simple main loop. This simplicity comes from the fact that we've encapsulated most of our logic in functions:

```python
def quit_game():
    pygame.quit()
    raise SystemExit

# main loop
while True:
    window.fill((255,255,255))
```

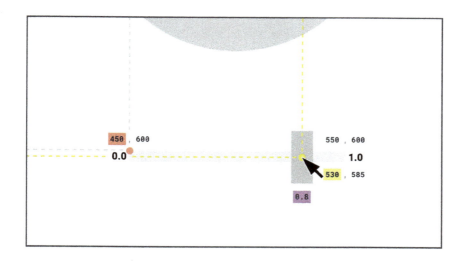

Figure 5-3 The equation used to control the volume

```
for event in pygame.event.get():
    if event.type == pygame.KEYDOWN:
        if event.key == pygame.K_ESCAPE:
            quit_game()
    if event.type == pygame.QUIT:
        quit_game()
    elif event.type == pygame.MOUSEBUTTONUP:
        handle_button_click()
    elif event.type == CLEAR_FLASH:
        flashed = None

draw_buttons()
update_volume()
draw_volume_slider()

pygame.display.update()
clock.tick(FPS)
```

And that's it. We've learned everything we need to know about making sounds play in our game. We've covered background audio, the sound mixer, streaming sound, and sound objects. We've also used lists and dictionaries to create and manipulate buttons, building on what we learned in the previous chapter. Now, we have a fully functioning soundboard which could form part of a game.

If you want a challenge, see if you can write code using what you've learned in the book so far to trigger the animal sounds using the keys 1-9 on your keyboard.

Chapter 6

Physics and forces

Let's give our game objects mass and simulate the effects of gravity on their movements

In previous chapters, we've put together code that let us take control of elements in our program whenever we interact with them, be it by clicking, dragging or typing. The difficulty is, there's only so much we can do with these interactions; no matter what, everything we do will be determined by ourselves in some way, and that can get a little bit boring after a while. This being the case, in this chapter we're going to give certain elements of our program the ability to interact with things around them without us having to do *anything*: we're going to add gravity (or rather, motion that really closely resembles gravity) to some planets that we're going to make as part of a solar system simulator.

We must acknowledge a debt of gratitude to Daniel Shiffman for the inspiration behind this chapter. His book *The Nature of Code* explains the concepts found here and more in far greater detail. All of his code is written in Processing (which itself is based on Java), but you should be able to convert it to Python with a little bit of work.

Understanding gravity

You may be thinking that we have already covered the subject of gravity in Chapter 3, *Take control: keyboard, mouse, and gamepad*. This is only partly the case. There, we added a force which we called gravity to certain objects to make them fall to the bottom of the window. However, that force was not particularly dynamic: no matter the object's size or velocity, it would simply add to the Y value of an object until it reached the bottom of the screen, which is not very interesting. For this new kind of gravity, we're going to be using vectors. You were introduced to a class called **Vector2** in Chapter 5, *Pygame Soundboard*, where we used that class to simplify mathematical operations on pairs of coordinates. In this chapter, we'll make more extensive use of them to model physics and forces.

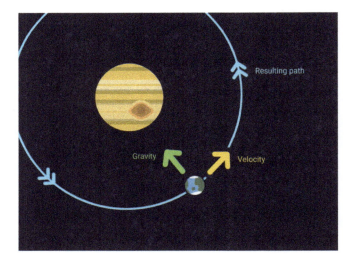

Figure 6-1   The gravitational attraction of two bodies, one orbiting the other

A vector (more specifically, a *Euclidean vector*) is a data structure that describes two things: *direction* and *magnitude*. With these, we can calculate the effect of one object with mass on the velocity (the speed and direction) of another object with mass. This program is bigger than anything we've made before, but we're not going to look at all of it in close detail. That's because you've already learned how to do most of the things, such as drawing images or handling key presses. Instead, we're going to focus on describing gravity and implementing that in our code.

So, what is this 'gravity' business, anyway?

In the real world, gravity describes how objects with mass attract one another. The force of that attraction follows a rule called the *inverse square law*, which applies to physical phenomena such as light, radiation, and gravity: the strength of the phenomenon is inversely proportional to the square of the distance from the source of the phenomenon. In the case of gravitational attraction between two objects, the strength is also directly proportional to the product of the two masses.

This seems like a very complicated concept, but what does it mean? It's actually really simple: it means the force acting on something reduces as the distance increases. Put simply, further away means less force, closer means more force.

Consider the Earth's pull on a football sitting on the ground, which is roughly 6,371,000 metres from Earth's centre of mass (Earth's radius). Now, suppose we moved that football 6,371,000 metres *above* Earth. Ignoring the effects of a near-vacuum on a football, we'd expect the force of gravity to be about one-quarter of what it was on earth. Why is that? Let's use x to represent the product of the football's mass, Earth's mass, and the gravitational constant. Let's simplify things even further by using R to represent Earth's radius.

In the case of the earthbound football, we'll multiply x by $1/R^2$. In the case of the high-altitude football, multiply x by $1/(2R)^2$. As it happens, $1/(2R)^2$ is equal to $1/R^2$ multiplied by ¼ (take out the R term, and you're comparing $1/2^2$ to $1/1^2$ or ¼ to 1).

To calculate the force of gravity in our simulation, we'll multiply the masses (in kilograms) of the two objects and divide that result by the square of distance (in metres) between their centres. In our universe, you'd also multiply the product of the masses by Newton's gravitational constant (represented as G). In our game's universe, we're defining G to be 10, which gives us the following formula:

`(10 * mass1 * mass2) / (distance ** 2)`

`**` is the exponent operator, so we're squaring the distance by raising it to the second power.

Another aspect of gravity is that it acts along a line between the centres of the objects. Gravity always pulls and never repels. It always pulls in the direction of the objects it is pulling. It is because of this truth that we're going to use vectors to simulate gravity. Using vectors, we can calculate the direction of each object in relation to another and adjust it to the force of gravitational attraction accordingly. The result is that gravity happens.

V is for vector

So now we've got an understanding of how gravity works, it's time to take a look at what a vector is. **Figure 6-2** illustrates several vectors but remember that Pygame's Y direction is the opposite of a Cartesian grid's: as Y values increase, Pygame coordinates move towards the bottom of the window.

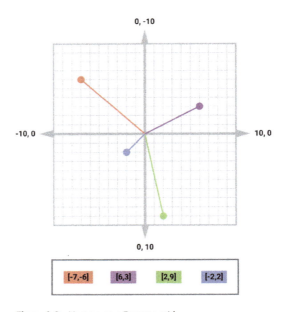

Figure 6-2   Vectors on a Pygame grid

You can think of a vector like an arrow: it has two values, an X and a Y, and together these point in a direction. For example, if we were to draw a line from (0,0) along a vector of (6, -3) on a grid, it would point up and to the right; for every unit travelled along the X axis (pixels, centimetres, inches, fathoms, the unit type doesn't matter), -0.5 units would be travelled along the Y axis. If we were to draw another line from (0,0) along a vector of (-2, 2), the line would travel to the left and down; for each unit travelled along the X axis, one would be traversed along the Y axis.

With vectors we can describe direction, but we can also express something called magnitude. The magnitude of the vector is the length of the line drawn between (0,0) and the vector on a grid, but we can also think of the magnitude as an amount or size of something; for example, we could use it as speed.

When we use vectors to describe direction, it often helps to normalise them. This means we take a vector, such as (1, 3) and turn each value into a value somewhere between -1 and 1 by dividing it by the vector's magnitude: in an application of the Pythagorean theorem, take the square of each coordinate, add them together, and take the square root of that sum. In the case of (1, 3), you'd calculate the square root of $1^2 + 3^2$ — the square root of 10, which is roughly 3.16.

So, the vector (1, 3) would be normalised to (0.316, 0.949), because 1/3.16 is 0.316 and 3/3.16 is roughly 0.949. (-8, 2.4) would normalise to (-0.958, 0.287). Normalising our values in this way makes it much easier to affect things with force and direction. By having a value between -1 and 1, we have only an indication of direction. When we have that, we're free to adjust it by any value to suit our needs; for instance, we could multiply the values by a speed value to give an object motion. **Figure 6-3** shows how you'd normalise some other vectors.

A speedy overview

To quickly recap: gravity always attracts in the direction of something with a mass; vectors describe a direction and a magnitude which is an amount of something, such as speed; and vectors can be collapsed to a value between -1 and 1 to describe only a direction through a process called *normalisation*. Now it's time to model gravity in Pygame.

As we said earlier, we're going to skip over explaining a lot of the code for this tutorial — it is all material we have looked at before — but for

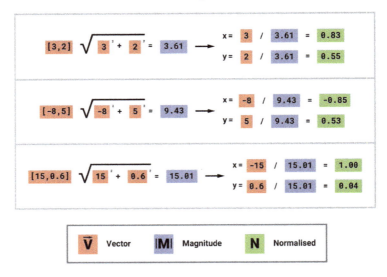

Figure 6-3 Calculating the magnitude of a vector and normalising it

the sake of clarity we'll do a quick pass over the functions, what they do, and the order they're called in. With the knowledge we've gained, we're going to construct a solar system simulator that moves planets around with gravity, based on their mass and velocity. The simulator has two parts: **solarsystem.py**, a library that contains metadata and a function for creating a new planet, and **simulator.py**, which contains all the simulator logic.

Planetary metadata

First, let's start with the metadata. In **solarsystem.py**, we define the planets as a dictionary with the planet names as the key, and a nested dictionary that contains the radius and mass. So, to get the mass of Mars, you'd write `PLANETS["mars"]["mass"]`.

```
import pygame
import copy
```

```python
from pygame.math import Vector2

# Planet data
PLANETS = {
    "mercury": {"radius": 15.0, "mass": 0.6},
    "venus":   {"radius": 23.0, "mass": 0.95},
    "earth":   {"radius": 24.0, "mass": 1.0},
    "mars":    {"radius": 15.0, "mass": 0.4},
    "jupiter": {"radius": 37.0, "mass": 15.0},
    "saturn":  {"radius": 30.0, "mass": 4.0},
    "neptune": {"radius": 30.0, "mass": 4.2},
    "uranus":  {"radius": 30.0, "mass": 3.8}
}
```

Next, we load all the planet images and store them in a dictionary called **IMAGES**. After that, we initialise the velocity and position for each planet. We could have put this in the definition of **PLANETS** earlier, but because the initial values are all empty **Vector2** objects, this is a little more compact and reduces repetition. Finally, we have a function named **make_new_planet()**, which we'll use in **simulator.py** when we want to add a new planet to our solar system. Before we return the new planet, we add that planet's image to the dictionary that represents the planet:

```python
# Load the planet images
IMAGES = {}
for name in PLANETS:
    IMAGES[name] = pygame.image.load(f"assets/{name}.png")

# Set starting position and velocity for each planet
for planet in PLANETS.values():
    planet["velocity"] = Vector2(0, 0)
    planet["pos"] = Vector2(0, 0)

def make_new_planet(name):
    planet = copy.deepcopy(PLANETS[name])
    planet["image"] = IMAGES[name]
    return planet
```

Setting up

At the top of **simulator.py** we have all of the familiar initialisation we need to run our program: initialising Pygame, setting up the window, and loading various image assets. The `import` statements at the top of our script are almost identical to our previous programs, with one exception: `import solarsystem`. You'll need those assets to run the code; check out the code from our GitHub repository (**rpimag.co/pygamebookgit**) and you'll find them in the **code/ch06/assets/** subdirectory, which is exactly where we want them.

```python
import pygame
import solarsystem
from pygame.math import Vector2

pygame.init()
clock = pygame.time.Clock()
FPS = 60

WIN_WIDTH = 1024
WIN_HEIGHT = 768
window = pygame.display.set_mode((WIN_WIDTH, WIN_HEIGHT))
pygame.display.set_caption('Solar System Simulator')

background = pygame.image.load("assets/background.jpg")
logo = pygame.image.load("assets/logo.png")
ui = pygame.image.load("assets/tabs.png")
```

Click here for planets

Next, we initialise some variables to help us draw the user interface (UI) on screen. This will be a collection of tabs, one for each planet. Users will create new planets by dragging a planet from the UI to the screen.

We calculate the UI's X position as one-half the difference between the window's width and the UI tab's width, which centres it. Its Y position is the window height minus the UI tab's height. These are stored into the **UI_POS** constant which represents the upper-left position of the UI. The **UI_SPACING** variable is the width of each planet (the UI width divided by the number of planets) plus a two-pixel offset for the gap between planets.

Next, we populate an array called **ui_coords**, which contains the click zones for each tab — we'll use those coordinates later to determine which tab the user clicked. In the **draw_ui()** function, which is called each time we redraw the screen, we draw the UI tab graphic and then draw each planet at its appropriate offset.

```python
# Initialise the user interface metadata
UI_POS = (int((WIN_WIDTH-ui.get_width())/2),
          WIN_HEIGHT-ui.get_height())
NUM_PLANETS = len(solarsystem.PLANETS)
UI_SPACING = int(ui.get_width()/NUM_PLANETS + 2)

ui_coords = []  # Name and location of each planet button
x = UI_POS[0]
for name in solarsystem.PLANETS:
    # Calculate the click zones for each tab
    ui_coords.append({"name": name,
                      "coords": (x + 1, UI_POS[1])})
    x += UI_SPACING

def draw_ui():
    global ui_coords

    window.blit(ui, UI_POS) # Draw the UI tab graphic
    x = UI_POS[0]
    for name in solarsystem.PLANETS:

        # Draw the planet on the tab
        rect = pygame.Rect(x, UI_POS[1],
                           ui.get_height(), ui.get_height())
        img = solarsystem.IMAGES[name]
        window.blit(img, img.get_rect(center=rect.center))
        x += UI_SPACING
```

The functions **draw_body()**, **draw_bodies()**, and **draw_current_body()** appear next. These are responsible for drawing the elements of our program to our window. Every time the main loop runs, we call **draw_ui()**, calculate the movement of the bodies, and then call **draw_bodies()**. If the user is dragging a planet around, we call **draw_current_body()**, which is responsible for drawing the planet until the user lets it go to affect other planets with its gravity.

```python
def draw_body(body):
    window.blit(body["image"],
                body["pos"] - Vector2(body["radius"]))

def draw_bodies():
    # Update the position of the bodies and draw them
    for p in bodies:
        p["pos"] += p["velocity"]
        draw_body(p)

def draw_current_body():
    current_body["pos"] = mouse_pos
    draw_body(current_body)
```

The movement of the Spheres

Next comes the **calculate_movement()** function. It is here that we make all of the gravity magic happen. It gets called in the main loop, just before **draw_bodies()**. No matter how far apart two objects are in the universe, they still have a gravitational pull on one another, even if it is infinitesimally small. If you were to place two dice a metre apart in space and leave them to their own devices, eventually the pull of the dice on one another would bring them both together without any help from another force. This effect is replicated in our simulator. Each planet in our solar system has a gravitational effect on every other body in our system. To do this, we create a **for** loop that works through every planet in our **bodies** list.

For each body we have, we want to calculate its effect on every other planet in our system, so the first thing the **for** loop does is create another loop to work through the rest of the planets (**other_bodies**). We don't want to calculate the effect of a planet on itself, so we exclude the current planet (**p**) when we construct the **other_bodies** array by adding `if x is not p` to the Python *list comprehension* we use to build the array.

Once we have a valid planet to affect (the variable **op**), we can start working with numbers and figuring out some vectors.

The first thing we need to find is the vector between the planet (**p**) and **op**. We do this with the variable **direction**, so named because it points from the coordinates of our planet to the coordinates of the other planet that we're trying to affect. Once we have the direction, we can work out the magnitude (in this case, the distance) between the two planets.

To help us work out the magnitude of our direction vector, we can use Pygame's built-in **distance_to()** function. It implements the actual formula for figuring out the magnitude, which we looked at back in "V is for vector" on page 82. However, if two objects are right atop each other, **magnitude** is zero, so we simply **continue** to the next iteration of the loop without doing anything (and thus avoiding a divide by zero error).

Next, we need to normalise our **direction** vector. Normalising our vector means we'll have vector **x** and **y** values that are proportional to one another but fall between -1 and 1. This is useful for us, because that lets us multiply our vector by any value we wish to apply to our force. To normalise our vector, we could divide our **direction** vector by **magnitude**, but Pygame provides us a **normalize()** function, and we store its result in the variable **n_direction**.

We have almost everything we need to start applying gravity, but before we do, we should limit **magnitude**. Strange things happen when forces are very big or very small, even in simulators, so we set a maximum for the number that magnitude can be. We combine calls to **max()** and **min()** to *clamp* the value of magnitude between 5 and 30.

We now have all we need to apply gravity to our planet. However, at this point, we'd be applying an arbitrary value that had nothing to do with the properties of our planets. What we want to do now is take into consideration the mass of our objects, because gravity only affects things with mass.

That's where the **strength** variable comes in. Here, we calculate how much force we need to apply to each planet to generate gravity. First, we multiply the planet's mass by the other planet's mass and multiply that by our **gravity** variable. The **gravity** value is arbitrary, and you can tweak it to generate stronger or weaker gravitational effects: remember, we're creating the illusion of gravity, not actually modelling the universe. Next, we divide that value by `clamped_mag` squared (`** 2` raises it to the second power, squaring it): this enables our objects to accelerate as they approach one another. Finally, we divide all that by the mass of the other planet (the one we're affecting). This lets our objects move slower if they are dense, and faster if they are less dense. By making it harder to move the big planets, we avoid small planets towing much larger ones around.

We now have the values we need to apply gravity to our planets. By multiplying our normalised direction vector (`n_direction`) by the `strength` value, we now have a vector (`applied_force`) with both direction and magnitude determined by the gravitational attraction of our objects. Finally, we subtract the applied force from the other planet's velocity. The next time that planet is drawn, its velocity will have been adjusted by gravity.

```python
def calculate_movement():
    for p in bodies:
        other_bodies = [x for x in bodies if x is not p]
        for op in other_bodies:
            # Difference in the X,Y coordinates of the planets
            direction = op["pos"] - p["pos"]

            # Distance between the two
            magnitude = op["pos"].distance_to(p["pos"])
            if magnitude == 0: # Two planets atop each other!
                continue

            # Normalised vector pointing in the
            # direction of the force
            n_direction = direction.normalize()

            # We need to limit the gravity to stop things
            # flying off to infinity... and beyond!
            clamped_mag = max(5, min(30, magnitude))

            # How strong should the attraction be?
            strength = ((gravity * p["mass"] * op["mass"]) /
                        (clamped_mag ** 2)) / op["mass"]
```

```
        applied_force = Vector2(n_direction * strength)

        op["velocity"] -= applied_force
        if draw_attractions:
            pygame.draw.line(window, (255,255,255),
                                  p["pos"], op["pos"], 1)
```

The last section of **calculate_movement()** doesn't have anything to do with moving the planets: it simply draws a line between our planet and every other planet that it's having an effect on, as shown in **Figure 6-4**. It's the line of attraction we looked at earlier, and it illustrates the directions that gravity is pulling our planets in. You can toggle this on and off with the **A** key.

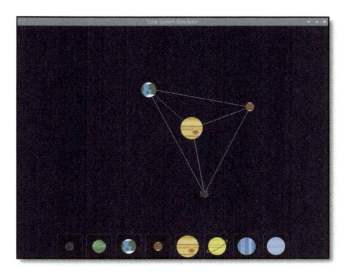

Figure 6-4   The lines of attraction drawn between planets

Tying it all together

The remaining functions handle the mouse and system events. When our player clicks somewhere in our window, **handle_mouse_down()** is run and checks whether or not our user clicked in one of the planet tabs at the bottom of our window with **check_ui_for_click()**. If they have, **check_ui_for_click()** will return the name of that planet and it will be created with **solarsystem.make_new_planet()**, the only function that we imported with **import solarsystem** at the start of our script. The **quit_game()** function does exactly what its name suggests.

```python
def check_ui_for_click(coords):
    h = ui.get_height()
    for tab in ui_coords:
        x = tab["coords"][0]
        if coords[0] >= x + 1 and coords[0] < x + h:
            return tab["name"]
    return False

def handle_mouse_down():
    global current_body

    if(mouse_pos[1] >= UI_POS[1]):
        name = check_ui_for_click(mouse_pos)

        if name:
            current_body = solarsystem.make_new_planet(name)

def quit_game():
    pygame.quit()
    raise SystemExit
```

Finally, we have some variables to keep track of what's going on in the simulator, followed by a main loop. Just like in our previous programs, it is from here that we call functions to handle user interactions and update our surface. The event loop is a little more involved than earlier ones, but we have more to do here. You'll notice that we're checking for a **KEYUP** event rather than using **pygame.key.get_pressed()**. **KEYUP** tells us when the key is released, which is what we're interested in when processing the reset (**R**) or toggle attractions (**A**) keys. If we just checked for key presses, we'd run the associated code over and over again until the key is released, and in the case of toggling attractions, it would be anyone's guess as to whether they are on or off when you finally release the key.

```python
prev_mouse_pos = Vector2()
mouse_pos = None
bodies = []
current_body = None
draw_attractions = True
gravity = 10.0
mouse_down = False
while True:

    for event in pygame.event.get():
        if event.type == pygame.KEYDOWN:
            if event.key == pygame.K_ESCAPE:
                quit_game()
        if event.type == pygame.KEYUP:
            if event.key == pygame.K_r:
                bodies = []
            if event.key == pygame.K_a:
                draw_attractions = not draw_attractions

        mouse_pos = Vector2(pygame.mouse.get_pos())
        if event.type == pygame.MOUSEBUTTONDOWN:
            mouse_down = True
            handle_mouse_down()
        if event.type == pygame.MOUSEBUTTONUP:
            mouse_down = False

        if event.type == pygame.QUIT:
            quit_game()
```

Still in the main loop, it's here where our simulator logic starts to appear. First, we do the usual job of drawing a background, and then we call the **draw_ui()**, **calculate_movement()**, and **draw_bodies()** functions.

After that, we check to see if there's a value in the **current_body** variable. If it is, it means that the user is dragging a planet around on screen and hasn't released it, so we call **draw_current_body()** to display it at the mouse cursor position. We then check the **mouse_down** variable, which will be **True** if the user is holding the mouse button down, **False** otherwise. If they released the mouse while **current_body** has a value, it means they just released the planet, so we set that body's velocity based on the current and previous mouse position (which means you can throw planets!), add the body to the **bodies** array, and set **current_body** to **None**. Finally, there's some code that keeps the logo on screen for the first four seconds, a variable to store the previous mouse position, and the usual calls to **clock.tick()** and to update the display.

```
window.blit(background, (0,0))

    # Draw the UI, update the movement of the bodies,
    # then draw the bodies in their new positions.
    draw_ui()
    calculate_movement()
    draw_bodies()

    # If our user has created a new planet,
    # draw it where the mouse is.
    if current_body:
        draw_current_body()

        # If they've released the mouse, add the new planet to
        # the bodies list and let gravity do its thing
        if not mouse_down:
            v = (mouse_pos - prev_mouse_pos) / 4
            current_body["velocity"] = v
            bodies.append(current_body)
            current_body = None

    # Draw the logo for the first four seconds of the program
    if pygame.time.get_ticks() < 4000:
        window.blit(logo, (108,77))

    # Store the previous mouse coordinates to create a vector
    # when we release a new planet
    prev_mouse_pos = mouse_pos

    clock.tick(FPS)
    pygame.display.update()
```

So, let's get to work making our own planets! If you fire up the **simulator.py** script, you'll see our Solar System Simulator. After four seconds, the logo will disappear. You can drag one of the eight planets at the bottom to somewhere on the screen. Each planet has characteristics which loosely reflect those of its real-world counterpart. Jupiter has the greatest mass, Mercury has the least, Venus is only slightly smaller than Earth, Mars is a third of Earth's size and so on. By clicking on a planet, we create a new planet which is stored in the **current_body** variable. The latter lets us create and place a planet without affecting any other planets on the screen. It's only when we let go of the planet that gravity is allowed to take effect on the new body in the solar system.

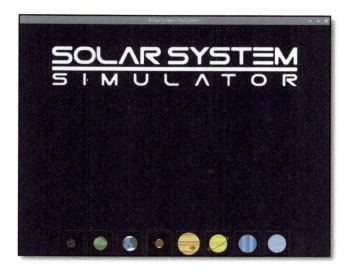

Figure 6-5   Our Solar System Simulator on its first run

Rounding up

We have covered rather a lot of material in this chapter. We have learned all about vectors and how we can use them to determine both speed and direction, rather like velocity. We have also learned how to normalise values so they can be made to do our bidding through multiplication. We have learned about how gravity works in the real world, and how we can emulate that in our simulated world. We also have some pretty neat code for handling mouse and keyboard events. It may have been complicated, but hopefully you are getting a sense of what you can do with Pygame.

Chapter 7

Physics and Collisions

What happens when a not-so-unstoppable force meets a not-so-immovable object? Let's create circles which bounce off one another

In Chapter 6, *Physics and forces*, we simulated a sizeable amount of a solar system. Using vectors and maths, we created a gravitational attraction between objects with mass to simulate their movement in space. Small objects would orbit larger ones, large objects would move very little when attracted to smaller objects and vice versa, and all was well in the simulated world. That said, one thing might have seemed a little odd: when two objects collide in the real world, they bounce off one another (or implode), but in our simulation they just slipped by one another as if they were ghosts. This time, however, we're going to write code that lets our objects collide and bounce off each other.

So, what are we making?

Unlike last time, we aren't going to be using planets and the solar system to prettify the effect — we're going to use basic circles for our program. Using circles makes it easier for us to use maths to calculate collisions, and we can change the properties of the circles to reflect the qualities they represent: for example, more mass or a bigger radius. That said, although we aren't using images of the solar system in this program, we can still think of the particles we'll be colliding in terms of a solar system.

The smallest of our 'collidable' objects will be like meteors: they move really fast, but require less energy to do so. A medium-size object would behave much as a planet might; they move at a moderate speed and have more kinetic energy behind them (see **Figure 7-1**). If they bump into a smaller object, they will adjust course, but not by much, whereas the smaller body will fly off!

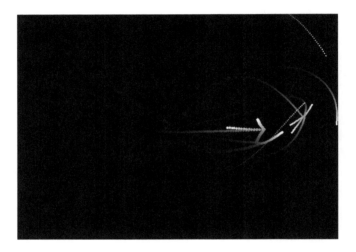

Figure 7-1 Simulating object collisions

We're going to use the code from the last chapter as a springboard for this one. Each object will have a mass and will attract every other object gravitationally using the same `calculateMovement()` method as before.

Let's take a quick walk through our code now. Just like our previous bits of code, the top of **collisions.py** imports the modules we'll need for our code and declares the variables that we'll be using throughout the tutorial. Obviously, these variables are very similar to the variables we used for our solar system simulator, but there's one little difference: instead of storing all of our planets in a list called `bodies`, this time we're storing all of our objects in the `collidables` list.

```python
import pygame
import math
import random
import itertools
from pygame.math import Vector2

pygame.init()
clock = pygame.time.Clock()
FPS = 60

WIN_WIDTH = 1024
WIN_HEIGHT = 768
window = pygame.display.set_mode((WIN_WIDTH, WIN_HEIGHT))
pygame.display.set_caption('Collisions')
```

The following functions will also seem familiar. **draw_collidables()** combines the logic of the **draw_planet()** and **draw_planets()** functions, and the **calculate_movement()** function, which handles gravity's effect on all our objects, is the same, except for some different variable names.

```python
def draw_collidables():
    for obj in collidables:
        obj["pos"] += obj["velocity"]
        pygame.draw.circle(window, obj["colour"],
                           obj["pos"], int(obj["radius"]), 0)

def calculate_movement():
    for o in collidables:
        other_objs = [x for x in collidables if x is not o]
        for other in other_objs:
            direction = other["pos"] - o["pos"]
            magnitude = other["pos"].distance_to(o["pos"])
            if magnitude == 0:
                continue
            n_direction = direction.normalize()

            clamped_mag = max(5, min(15, magnitude))

            strength = ((gravity * o["mass"] * other["mass"]) /
                        (clamped_mag ** 2)) / other["mass"]
```

```
        applied_force = Vector2(n_direction * strength)
        other["velocity"] -= applied_force

    if draw_attractions:
        pygame.draw.line(window, (255,255,255),
                         o["pos"], other["pos"], 1)
```

The **draw_current_object()** is similar to the one you saw in Chapter 6, *Physics and forces*, in that it draws the new object you are creating at the mouse cursor position. The big difference is that if you hold the left mouse button down, the object will change in size: the longer you hold the mouse button down, the bigger it gets. If the object exceeds the maximum allowed radius, it starts shrinking until it gets down to a radius of 1, when it starts growing again. The **if not (1 < current_obj["radius"] < 20)** line may look a little strange, but it's basically saying that if the current object's radius is not between 1 and 20, then we need to reverse the sign of the expansion variable. Each time **draw_current_object()** is called, the radius increases by the amount of the expansion, and the object is drawn, in red, on the screen. This function is only called while the mouse button is held down, so as long as you're doing just that, you can move the object around on screen and change its size.

```
def draw_current_object():
    global current_obj, expansion

    current_obj["pos"] = mouse_pos

    # If we've exceeded either bound, reverse the expansion
    if not (1 < current_obj["radius"] < 20):
        expansion *= -1

    # Increase the radius by the expansion factor, and set
    # the mass equal to the radius.
    current_obj["radius"] += expansion
    current_obj["mass"] = current_obj["radius"]

    pygame.draw.circle(window, (255,0,0),
                       current_obj["pos"],
                       int(current_obj["radius"]), 0)
```

The `handle_collisions()` function is where we'll spend most of our time in this tutorial. Here, we check for colliding objects and adjust their trajectories accordingly.

What do we need to know to simulate a collision?

We need to know a couple of things before we can simulate a collision. First, we need to know which two objects, if any, are colliding. Once we know which two objects are colliding, we need to figure out how fast they're going, the angle of incidence (which we'll look at in a little while), and the mass of each of the objects.

> **THANKS**
>
> A hat tip for this chapter goes out to Steve and Jeff Fulton. They put a huge amount of effort into dissecting old Flash-based physics code into its core parts and putting it back together for their book *HTML Canvas*, which made this chapter possible.

So, how do we know which two objects are colliding? This is pretty straightforward when you use circles. Circles are regular shapes: each point along the circumference is the same distance from the centre as every other point; this measurement from the edge to the centre is the radius. By measuring the distance between the centres of two objects, we can check whether or not the outlines of the objects are intersecting. If the distance between the centres of two circles is less than the radius of each circle added to the other, we can conclude that they must be colliding, as shown in **Figure 7-2**.

In `calculate_movement()`, we ran through each pair of objects twice: each time through the loop, we only adjusted the velocity of the second object in the pair (we'd process the first object's influence on the second, then vice-versa on a subsequent loop iteration). In `handle_collisions()`, we'll calculate the change in velocity for both objects for each iteration, so we only want to look at each pair once.

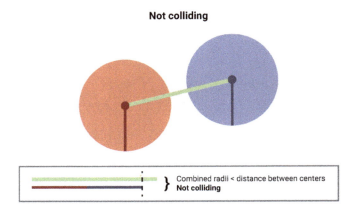

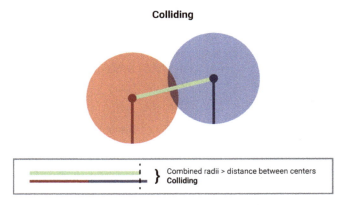

Figure 7-2 All the aspects needed to bounce one circle off another

At the top of the function, we use **itertools.combinations()** with a **for** loop to work through every possible pair of collidable objects in our simulation. Unlike the **itertools.product()** function we used in Chapter 5, *Pygame Soundboard*, the order of elements of each pair is not significant, so we only process every unique pair, not every possible pair. For example, **itertools.product([1,2,3], repeat=2)** would yield (1, 1), (1, 2), (1, 3), (2, 1), and so forth while **itertools.combinations([1,2,3], 2)** would yield only (1, 2), (1, 3), and (2, 3).

Inside this loop, we measure the distance between the centres of every pair of objects in our **collidables** list. We do this with our **distance** variable, using Pygame's **distance_to()** function. If the distance between the two centres of our objects is more than the combined length of the radius of each circle, our objects are not colliding, and we then continue on measuring the distance to other circles. However, if the distance is less than the sum of the radii, then our objects are colliding, and we can start figuring out what to do with them.

```
def handle_collisions():
    for (o, other) in itertools.combinations(collidables, 2):

        distance = other["pos"].distance_to(o["pos"])
        if distance < other["radius"] + o["radius"]:
```

All the rest of the code in **handle_collisions()** is nested under that **if** function. If it evaluates to **False**, the code moves on to the next iteration of the loop.

The angle of incidence

How do we create a convincing bounce effect? In the past, whenever we've wanted to restrict or adjust movement, we've been doing so with squares or rectangles — shapes with flat sides. Going too much to the right? OK, we'll send it back to the left. Going too far down? OK, we'll send it back up. Now, we're dealing with circles. Instead of having eight directions to choose from, we now have 360. If our circles hit each other square on, then all we have to do is send them back along the path they came, but these are circles with gravity; hitting another circle directly along the X or Y axis is not going to happen very often. If a collision happens a little to the left or right of the centre of the X or Y axis, we need to send our objects on two new paths, but how do we know which direction to send each object? For this, we need to use the *angle of incidence*: this is the angle at which an object is travelling as it collides with another object. If we know the angle at which two things collide, we can figure out along which angle we can send them on their way onward: this is the *angle of reflection*, which is the reverse of the angle of incidence.

This is not as complicated as it sounds. Imagine a ball hitting a vertical wall at an angle 45 degrees, so its vector is (1, 1), travelling to the right and down in equal measure. After the ball hits the wall, the rate at which it falls to the ground is unchanged, but the direction it's travelling is reversed along its X axis; our ball is still travelling at 45 degrees, but now it's travelling away from the wall, at -45 degrees or with a vector of (-1, 1).

On the first line of code nested under the **if** statement at the end of the previous listing, we calculate the angle of incidence between the centre of the two circles colliding with **math.atan2()**, which basically works out the hypotenuse of an imaginary right-angled triangle drawn using the two centre points of the circles (see **Figure 7-3**). If you were to print out the value of the direction variable, you might expect it to read somewhere between 0 and 360 because an angle is measured in degrees. In fact, you'll get a value between 1 and 2π (**pi * 2**): our angle has been measured in radians. This may seem counter-intuitive, but to a computer (and mathematicians) it makes perfect sense. If you want to see the degree value, you can simply do **radians * (180/pi)**, which **Figure 7-4** illustrates, but we are going to stick with radians because it keeps our code tidy. Note that we flip the sign of the y component because Pygame's y axis is the opposite of the typical Cartesian grid that the **math** library functions expect.

```
# Angle of the collision between the two
coll = o["pos"] - other["pos"]
coll_angle = math.atan2(-coll.y, coll.x)
```

Bounce!

Now we've got the angle of incidence, we can calculate which way to send our colliding objects, but first we need to obtain a couple of other values to make everything work. Next, we need to work out the speed at which our circles are moving. You may wonder why, if we have vectors, we need a separate speed value. It is indeed true that we use vectors to affect the speed and direction of our objects, but that's part of the problem: our vector is a measure of both speed *and* direction. As it is, we can't use it to find out how many pixels our objects travel per frame; we need to separate the speed from the direction so we can perform some maths specific to each.

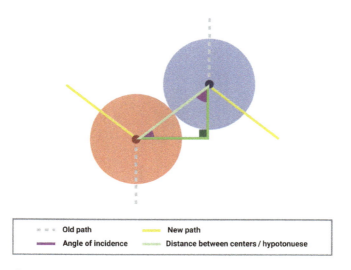

Figure 7-3   A right-angled triangle helps calculate the angle of incidence

Fortunately, we can use maths to figure out the speed of our objects — which we do on the following lines, one variable for each object in the collision — and the direction each object is moving in radians.

```python
# Calculate the speed of each object
obj_speed = o["velocity"].magnitude()
other_speed = other["velocity"].magnitude()

# Get direction of the objects in radians
obj_dir = math.atan2(-o["velocity"].y,
                     o["velocity"].x)
other_dir = math.atan2(-other["velocity"].y,
                       other["velocity"].x)
```

Now we have the speed and direction of each circle, we can adjust them separately to create the bouncing effect. First, we want to reverse the direction in which the objects are travelling, so we create a couple of variables to calculate new velocities. We recombine the speed and direction variables of each object to create new speeds for the **x** and **y** values of our circles. When used together, we have our new vector. But these ones will

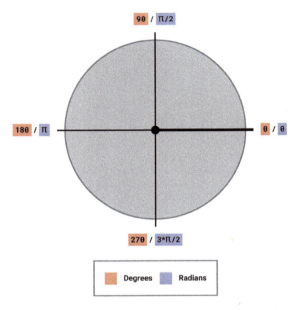

Figure 7-4 Angles on a circle and their equivalent values in radians

point our objects in the opposite direction of the angle of incidence — the angle of reflection. We've got the basics of our bounce.

```
# Calculate the post-collision velocity
obj_angle = obj_dir - coll_angle
obj_new_ang = Vector2(math.cos(obj_angle),
                      math.sin(obj_angle))
obj_new_vel = obj_new_ang * obj_speed

other_angle = other_dir - coll_angle
other_new_ang = Vector2(math.cos(other_angle),
                        math.sin(other_angle))
other_new_vel = other_new_ang * other_speed
```

Motion

Energy cannot be destroyed, only converted from one form to another. Motion is a form of energy and when two objects collide, an energy transfer happens between them. Of the two objects colliding, the faster object will transfer energy into the slower object, speeding the slower object up and slowing itself down. The two objects will move off in different directions and at different speeds than they were travelling before the collision, but the net energy of motion (the total amount of energy moving the objects) will remain exactly the same; it's just in different quantities in different objects now.

As we reach the end of the function, we take into consideration each object's mass and speed. The result is that bigger objects will take more energy to change direction than smaller ones. With this in place, we won't have large objects being sent off at high velocities by much smaller, faster-moving objects. Our physics model does not capture real-world physics exactly, and favours entertainment value over accuracy — for example, objects always bounce off each other in our model in contrast to the more accurate model shown in **Figure 7-5**. You can experiment with these values in an online calculator such as **rpimag.co/momentum_calc**.

> **MIX AND MATCH**
>
> We haven't used the planet graphics or much of the user interaction code that we wrote for the solar system, but, with a little work, you should be able to drop the `handleCollisions()` function into last chapter's code and make your planets bounce. Consider it a challenge!

Now we have the new vectors for our colliding objects, all we have to do is apply them to our objects. We're only going to apply the **x** values we've calculated to each object. If we applied both the adjusted **x** and **y** values to each object, they would bounce and follow the path they came along. That would be like throwing a ball and having it bounce straight back into your hand: it would be unnatural. By only applying the **x** value to our colliding objects, we create a convincing, bouncing, deflecting effect.

```
# Adjust velocity based on object masses
mass = o["mass"]
other_mass = other["mass"]
```

```python
    obj_final_vel = (
        ((mass - other_mass) * obj_new_vel
            + (other_mass * 2) * other_new_vel)
        / (mass + other_mass)
    )
    other_final_vel = (
        ((mass * 2) * obj_new_vel
            + (other_mass - mass) * other_new_vel)
        / (mass + other_mass)
    )

    # Set the final velocities
    o["velocity"].x = obj_final_vel.x
    other["velocity"].x = other_final_vel.x
```

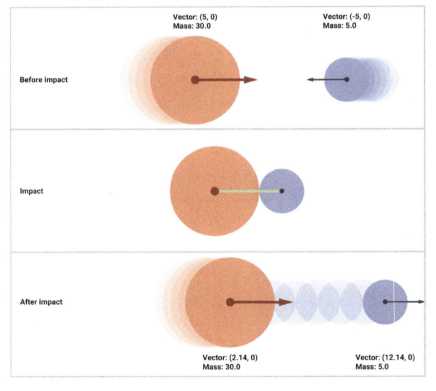

Figure 7-5 The effect of mass on vectors in a collision

And that's it: we can simply repeat this for every possible collidable object in our simulator.

The rest of the code contains the logic for our keyboard and mouse interactions, as well as some housekeeping variables and our main loop. Just as before, clicking in our window will create a new particle which will only affect the movement of other particles once the mouse button has been released. If the mouse was moving when it was released, the particle will inherit the velocity of the mouse pointer.

```python
def handle_mouse_down():
    global current_obj, expansion

    # Initialise a new circle and set current_obj to it.
    current_obj = {
        "radius" : 3,
        "mass" : 3,
        "velocity" : Vector2(),
        "pos" : Vector2(),
        "colour" : random.choices(range(256), k=3)
    }
    expansion = 0.2

def quit_game():
    pygame.quit()
    raise SystemExit

# main loop
prev_mouse_pos = Vector2()
mouse_pos = None
mouse_down = False
collidables = []
current_obj = None
draw_attractions = False
gravity = 1.0
expansion = 0.2
while True:

    # Handle events
    for event in pygame.event.get():
```

```python
        if event.type == pygame.KEYDOWN:
            if event.key == pygame.K_ESCAPE:
                quit_game()
        if event.type == pygame.KEYUP:
            if event.key == pygame.K_r:
                collidables = []
            if event.key == pygame.K_a:
                draw_attractions = not draw_attractions

        mouse_pos = Vector2(pygame.mouse.get_pos())
        if event.type == pygame.MOUSEBUTTONDOWN:
            mouse_down = True
            handle_mouse_down()
        if event.type == pygame.MOUSEBUTTONUP:
            mouse_down = False

        if event.type == pygame.QUIT:
            quit_game()

    window.fill((0,0,0))
    calculate_movement()
    handle_collisions()
    draw_collidables()

    if current_obj:
        draw_current_object()

        # If our user has released the mouse, add the new obj
        # to the collidables list and let gravity do its thing
        if not mouse_down:
            v = (mouse_pos - prev_mouse_pos) / 4
            current_obj["velocity"] = v
            collidables.append(current_obj)
            current_obj = None

    # Store the previous mouse coordinates to create a vector
    # when we release a new obj
    prev_mouse_pos = mouse_pos
```

```
clock.tick(FPS)
pygame.display.update()
```

Now you're ready to give it a try. Run the program, and click (and hold) anywhere in the window to start creating a new object. Add a few circles to the simulation, and watch as they bounce off one another!

Figure 7-6 Use the mouse to create a new moving object

Chapter 8

Fred's Bad Day

Have your own bad day in this pulse-pounding sprite-powered barrel-dodging game

We are now over three quarters of the way through this book, which you can look at in two ways: on one hand, we are drawing close to the end, but on the other, we still have several opportunities to learn and make something amazing. We've put together so much already at this point: we've learned all about how Pygame draws shapes and images, how we can manipulate sounds and control events with our keyboards and mouse, we've made buttons and start screens and created floors that travel too quickly. We even built a solar system with gravity, which is no mean feat. Everything, however, has been leading up to one challenge: a final game, which we'll be making in the final two chapters.

We introduced the `Sprite` class back in Chapter 4, *Your first game*, but we haven't used it in subsequent chapters. Before we move on to our final game, let's reacquaint ourselves with `Sprite` and learn a few new tricks.

Fred is our game avatar. He works from nine to five in a barrel factory that, frankly, flouts health and safety regulations in its careless storage of barrels in overhead containers. Fred is a simple fellow, so much so that we can describe everything about him in a Python class — but there's only one Fred; nobody else would ever agree to the monotonous labour of the barrel factory. Fred is a one-off.

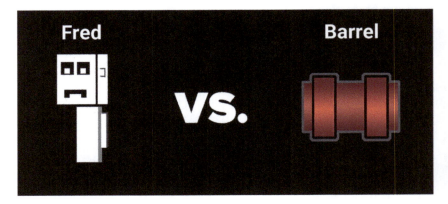

Figure 8-1   On the left is Fred. He's our game avatar and there's only one Fred. On the right is a barrel. There are many like it, but this one is ours

Our **Fred** class lives in the **objects.py** file of our project, so at the top of **freds_bad_day.py**, we `import objects` along with Pygame, followed by some familiar initialisation and setup. The background image is relatively large, so we call `convert()` on it to convert it into a format that will `blit()` faster. There's no harm in running `convert()` on all images that you load, but it's not strictly necessary.

```
import pygame
import objects

pygame.init()
pygame.font.init()
clock = pygame.time.Clock()
FPS = 60

WIN_WIDTH = 1000
WIN_HEIGHT = 768
FRED_OFFSET = 23
window = pygame.display.set_mode((WIN_WIDTH, WIN_HEIGHT))
pygame.display.set_caption("Fred's Bad Day")
textFont = pygame.font.SysFont("monospace", 50)

start_screen = pygame.image.load("assets/startgame.png")
```

```
end_screen = pygame.image.load("assets/gameover.png")
bg_img = pygame.image.load("assets/background.png").convert()
```

The **objects.py** file (which we'll look at in a little bit) contains our **Fred** and our **Barrel** sprites. Before we get into the functions and main loop that make up our game, we set some state variables, set up a **NEW_BARREL** event that we'll use to spawn barrels, and create Fred and a sprite group called **barrels**.

We're using **Fred** to refer to the Fred sprite class, and **fred** (all lower-case) to refer to an instance of **Fred** (our Fred). This is in keeping with Python coding guidelines. Out of respect, we'll refer to our Fred with the correct spelling of his name in the text, but in code, he'll be lower-case **fred**.

```
game_started = False
start_time = 0
time_lasted = 0
barrel_delay = 1500
NEW_BARREL = pygame.USEREVENT + 0

fred = objects.Fred(WIN_WIDTH, WIN_HEIGHT, FRED_OFFSET)
barrels = pygame.sprite.Group()
```

Notice that we passed the window width and height as arguments to **Fred()**. This will allow Fred to make decisions about where to appear in the main game window, and to avoid moving beyond the window's bounds. We also pass in an offset for Fred (defined as 23 earlier). This is because the 'ground' in the game background is 23 pixels above the bottom of the window. Fred will use this offset to decide where to stand.

After this, we have three functions to support the game logic. The **restart_game()** function sets the game to its initial state: it calls Fred's **reset()** function to configure his starting attributes such as health, position, and direction he's facing. It then destroys any barrels that might be in the sprite group. After that, it sets the **barrel_delay** to its default, sets a timer for spawning new barrels, and sets the **game_started** flag and the **start_time** variable.

Much to Fred's dismay, there's more than one barrel in the world. A new barrel is created after a certain amount of time passes (this amount of time gets smaller as the game progresses). The **new_barrel()** function creates a new barrel and adds it to the sprite group. It then decreases the barrel delay (unless it's already less than 150 milliseconds) and resets the timer. The **quit_game()** function is the same as the one you've seen in previous chapters.

```python
def restart_game():
    global game_started, start_time, barrels, barrel_delay

    fred.reset()
    for barrel in barrels:
        barrel.kill()

    barrel_delay = 1500
    pygame.time.set_timer(NEW_BARREL, barrel_delay)

    game_started = True
    start_time = pygame.time.get_ticks()

def new_barrel():
    global barrels, barrel_delay

    new_barrel = objects.Barrel(WIN_WIDTH, WIN_HEIGHT)
    barrels.add(new_barrel)
    if barrel_delay > 150:
        barrel_delay -= 50
    pygame.time.set_timer(NEW_BARREL, barrel_delay)

def quit_game():
    pygame.quit()
    raise SystemExit
```

The gameplay is handled by the aptly named **have_a_bad_day()**. We draw the gameplay background, check for key presses (left or right arrow) and set Fred's direction accordingly. After that, we update Fred and the **barrels** sprite group and then ask Fred to check whether he's collided with members of the sprite group. If, after that, Fred's health has dropped to **0** or less, we store the amount of time that Fred survived in **time_lasted**. If you're not familiar with the **//** operator, it behaves exactly as the division (**/**) operator, but always returns the result rounded down to the nearest integer, saving us the need to invoke **int()** on the result. After that, we draw the barrels and use **blit()** to draw Fred and his health meter.

```python
def have_a_bad_day():
    global time_lasted

    window.blit(bg_img, (0, 0))

    # Set Fred's direction based on the keys pressed
    pressed_keys = pygame.key.get_pressed()
    if pressed_keys[pygame.K_LEFT]:
        fred.set_direction(-1)
    elif pressed_keys[pygame.K_RIGHT]:
        fred.set_direction(1)

    fred.update()
    barrels.update()

    # Check for collisions and check Fred's health
    fred.check_collisions(barrels)
    if fred.health <= 0:
        time_tick = pygame.time.get_ticks()
        time_lasted = (time_tick - start_time) // 1000

    # Draw the barrels, Fred, and the health meter
    barrels.draw(window)
    window.blit(fred.image, fred.rect)
    window.blit(fred.health_meter(), (0, WIN_HEIGHT - 10))
```

The logic in the main loop is relatively simple. As usual, we check for events. There are two ways to quit the game: pressing the **ESC** key or closing the window. If the user presses **RETURN** or **ENTER**, the game will be restarted only if the **game_started** flag is **False**, or Fred's health is less than or equal to **0**. This works because the **game_started** flag is initialised to **False** when you first launch the game, then becomes — and remains — **True** after the first play. If the **NEW_BARREL** event is triggered by its timer, and so long as Fred's health is greater than zero, we call the **new_barrel()** function (after Fred's demise, there's no point in spawning more barrels).

After that, there are three states to the game, and what we do depends on which state we're currently in: upon first launching the game, `game_started` will be `False`. In this state, we should display the start screen. We're in the second state (game on!) when `game_started` is `True` and Fred's health is greater than zero. `have_a_bad_day()` handles everything in this state. The final state is the end game: if Fred's health has dropped to zero or lower, we draw the end screen and display how long he survived (in seconds).

```python
while True:
    for event in pygame.event.get():
        if event.type == pygame.KEYDOWN:
            if event.key == pygame.K_ESCAPE:
                quit_game()
            elif event.key == pygame.K_RETURN:
                if not game_started or fred.health <= 0:
                    restart_game()

        if event.type == pygame.QUIT:
            quit_game()
        if event.type == NEW_BARREL and fred.health > 0:
            new_barrel()

    # If the game hasn't been started, show the start screen
    if not game_started:
        window.blit(start_screen, (0, 0))

    # If the game is started and Fred's alive, play the game
    elif game_started and fred.health > 0:
        have_a_bad_day()

    # If Fred's health falls to 0, it's game over!
    elif fred.health <= 0:
        window.blit(end_screen, (0, 0))
        renderedText = textFont.render(f"{time_lasted:02}",
                                    1, (175,59,59))
        window.blit(renderedText, (495, 430))

    pygame.display.update()
    clock.tick(FPS)
```

This is Fred

'We are all stardust'… except for Fred. He's a class that inherits from Pygame's `Sprite` class. Fred's class is the blueprint for his existence, and it defines him at his most basic. As we've said, classes are great when you need to control loads of the same but slightly different things, but classes are also great for abstracting (or hiding away) bits of code that we use a lot but aren't useful everywhere and aren't used all of the time.

At the top of **objects.py**, we import `pygame`, `random`, and the `Vector2` class. After that, we see the beginning of Fred's class definition. It starts out with some class constants that any instance of Fred would need (maximum health, images, and speed). Next, we come to the `__init__()` method, Fred's constructor. We call the `__init__()` method from the superclass (`pygame.sprite.Sprite`) and then set Fred's image to the default, and Fred's `rect` property to that of his image. Finally, we store the three constructor arguments (`win_width`, `win_height`, and `y_offset`) in Fred's instance variables. As you saw earlier in **freds_bad_day.py**, we passed in the value of `FRED_OFFSET` as the `y_offset`.

At the end of the constructor, we call Fred's `reset()` function to set his default attributes. It positions Fred at the centre of the window with his feet planted at an offset from the bottom of the window (the offset corresponds to the height of the 'ground' drawn on the background image. The `reset()` function takes care of setting his game state variables, which include whether Fred was hit recently, when he was hit, his height, and the direction he's facing.

```python
import pygame
import random
from pygame.math import Vector2

class Fred(pygame.sprite.Sprite):
    MAX_HEALTH = 100
    DEFAULT_IMG = pygame.image.load("assets/Fred-Right.png")
    HIT_IMG = pygame.image.load("assets/Fred-Right-Hit.png")
    SPEED = 8

    def __init__(self, win_width, win_height, y_offset):
        super().__init__()
```

```python
        # Set initial image and rect
        self.image = self.DEFAULT_IMG
        self.rect = self.image.get_rect()

        self.window_dims = Vector2(win_width, win_height)
        self.y_offset = y_offset
        self.reset()

    def reset(self):
        self.rect.centerx = self.window_dims.x // 2
        self.rect.bottom = self.window_dims.y - self.y_offset

        self.is_hit = False
        self.time_hit = 0
        self.health = self.MAX_HEALTH
        self.direction = 1    # 0 = left, 1 = right
```

Next come Fred's **set_direction()** and **check_collision()** methods. The **set_direction()** function takes an argument, **direction**, which should be **1** or **-1**. It sets his direction property to that value and then multiplies his speed by his direction to figure out how much his X position should change. If he's within the bounds of the screen, it sets his X position to the new value; otherwise, it doesn't change it at all.

One of the clever things about Fred (and about classes as a whole) is that once we've instantiated him, we can pass him (or any other class instance) to other classes and functions as we like. When we call **check_collision()**, we pass the sprite group **barrels** as an argument. It uses Pygame's **spritecollideany()** function to find the first barrel that's collided with him. We're using a special version of the assignment operator (**:=**), sometimes called the walrus operator due to its resemblance to a certain marine mammal's eyes and tusks. It assigns the results of an expression and evaluates its value all in one go. If **spritecollideany()** returned a **Sprite**, it gets assigned to **b**, and the **if** statement proceeds.

If that barrel isn't already broken, it calls the barrel's **split()** function, sets Fred's **is_hit** property to **True**, records the time of the hit in his **time_hit** property, and deducts 10 points from his health. The reason we must make sure the barrel isn't already split is that in all likelihood, Fred will keep colliding with a broken barrel as it continues its fall. In that case, we don't want to keep deducting 10 points from his health because the game would end quite quickly if we did!

```python
def set_direction(self, direction):
    self.direction = direction
    # Make sure Fred remains within bounds before moving
    left_max = 0
    right_max = self.window_dims.x
    next_x = self.rect.x + self.SPEED * self.direction
    if left_max < next_x < right_max - self.rect.width:
        self.rect.x = next_x

def check_collisions(self, barrels):
    if b := pygame.sprite.spritecollideany(self, barrels):
        if not b.is_broken:
            b.split()
            self.is_hit = True
            self.time_hit = pygame.time.get_ticks()
            self.health -= 10
```

Fred's final two methods are **update()** and **health_meter()**. The **update()** method will update Fred's appearance.

If Fred was hit recently, we use a different image for Fred (the bottommost Fred who is frowning in **Figure 8-2**). Otherwise, we use the default image (the topmost Fred). If Fred's direction is **-1**, we flip the image along the X axis so that Fred faces the other direction. The last two arguments **pygame.transform.flip()** control whether to flip along the X or Y axis, respectively. The **health_meter()** method returns a **Surface** object that is a reddish health bar whose length is proportional to Fred's health: if Fred's health is 100, the meter will span the width of the window. That's it for Fred! Let's have a look at his arch-enemy next.

```python
def update(self):
    time = pygame.time.get_ticks()
    # Handle hit state timeout
    if self.is_hit and time - self.time_hit > 800:
        self.time_hit = 0
        self.is_hit = False
```

```python
        # Update sprite image based on hit state
        if self.is_hit:
            self.image = self.HIT_IMG
        else:
            self.image = self.DEFAULT_IMG
        # Flip the image if Fred is facing left
        if self.direction == -1:
            self.image = pygame.transform.flip(self.image,
                                               True, False)

    def health_meter(self):
        health_percentage = self.health / self.MAX_HEALTH
        surf = pygame.Surface((health_percentage
                               * self.window_dims.x, 10))
        surf.fill((175,59,59))
        return surf
```

Figure 8-2 A barrel splitting when it hits Fred

This is Fred's nemesis

Alan Ford's iconic character Brick Top, asked (and answered) a question in Guy Ritchie's *Snatch* (2000): "Do you know what nemesis means? A righteous infliction of retribution manifested by an appropriate agent."

The common barrel is the blight of Fred's life, it's Fred's nemesis. He spends his day shift running left to right and back again, cursing whichever middle-manager it was who thought storing a seemingly unlimited supply of barrels 20 feet above the ground would be a risk-free idea. Unlike Fred, there are many barrels, but at their core, they're both the same. `Fred` and `Barrel` are both classes, but Fred is only instantiated once, whereas our barrel is instantiated potentially hundreds of times (depending on how bad Fred's day is).

Like `Fred`, `Barrel` has some constants at the top of its class definition, a variable to track the last slot where a barrel appears, and a curious array named `slots`, which determines the locations on screen where a barrel might appear from. We don't want our barrels to be able to appear just anywhere; instead, we want them to appear in one of the 13 slots at the top of our game.

You'll see that `slots` is calculated as a series of alternating rows: the odd-numbered rows are those whose index divided by 2 leaves a remainder of 1, thanks to the modulo (`%`) operator. All the others are even-numbered. The X index of each slot appears every 76 pixels (after an initial offset of 4 pixels), and the Y index is either 51 or 128, depending on whether it's an odd- or even-numbered row. If you look at the **assets/background.png** image, you'll see that this spacing corresponds to the barrel slots drawn on the background image.

After that, we come to `Barrel`'s constructor. This sets the barrel's image, gets the `rect` from the image and stores it into the barrel's `rect` property. Then it picks a random slot until it finds one that's not equal to the last barrel slot and assigns the `rect`'s `x` and `y` property to that slot. After that, it stores the window dimensions that were passed in, sets the barrel's `is_broken` state to `False`, and its Y velocity to `1.5`.

```python
class Barrel(pygame.sprite.Sprite):
    BARREL_IMG = pygame.image.load("assets/Barrel.png")
    BROKEN_IMG = pygame.image.load("assets/Barrel_break.png")
    GRAVITY = 1.05
    MAX_Y = 20
    last_barrel_slot = 0

    # Calculate slot positions; these correspond to the slots
    # that are predrawn on the background image
    slots = []
    for i in range(13):
        if i % 2 == 1:
            y = 51
        else:
            y = 128
        slots.append((4 + (i * 76), y))
    last_barrel_slot = 0

    def __init__(self, win_width, win_height):
        super().__init__()

        self.image = Barrel.BARREL_IMG
        self.rect = self.image.get_rect()

        while True:
            slot = random.randint(0, 12)
            if slot != Barrel.last_barrel_slot:
                break
        Barrel.last_barrel_slot = slot
        self.rect.x = self.slots[slot][0]
        self.rect.y = self.slots[slot][1]
        self.window_dims = Vector2(win_width, win_height)

        self.is_broken = False
        self.vy = 1.5
```

BASH! CRASH! THUMP!

Now we come to the **split()** method. This sets the barrel's **is_broken** property to **True**, changes its Y velocity to **5**, and moves it ten pixels to the left. It also sets its image to that of a broken barrel. The **update()** method increases the barrel's velocity as it falls and applies its velocity.

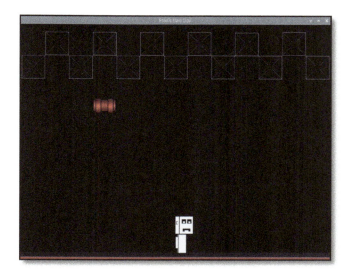

Figure 8-3 Like so many games, this one starts out easy

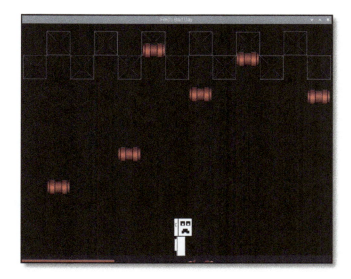

Figure 8-4 Before too long, it's raining barrels!

When a barrel hits poor Fred, it splits in two and continues to fall off the screen. Whether it hits Fred or not, when our barrel goes off screen, we should delete it, because we no longer need it, and it's eating up Python's resources. It would be ideal if our barrel could self-destruct, as it were, and remove itself from our game. Because the barrel knows the dimensions of its window, it can check to see whether it's exceeded those bounds in the **update()** method. If it has, it calls the sprite's own **kill()** function, which removes it from the sprite group (because this is the last reference to the barrel, Python's garbage collector will eventually delete it).

```python
def split(self):
    self.is_broken = True
    self.vy = 5
    self.rect.x -= 10
    self.image = Barrel.BROKEN_IMG

def update(self):
    # Apply gravity and movement
    if self.vy < Barrel.MAX_Y:
        self.vy = self.vy * Barrel.GRAVITY
    self.rect.y += self.vy

    # Remove if off screen
    if self.rect.y > self.window_dims.y:
        self.kill()
```

Recap

We've done a lot in this chapter, so let's recap before we build our space shooter game in the next chapter. We reacquainted ourselves with the `Sprite` class and learned a bit more about classes, which help keep our code tidy and reusable. We used Pygame's sprite collision facility to figure out when our hero has collided with a barrel, and we've added a user interface element to let us keep track of our hero's health.

In the remaining chapters, we are going to use absolutely everything we've learned so far to make an exciting space shooter game. There will be spaceships, lasers, gravity, sound effects, and all sorts of other thrills and spills. You'll love it!

Chapter 9

The Aliens Are Trying to Kill Me!

Let's make the first half of our final game project, putting to use everything we've learned so far

We have covered a wealth of material on the subject of making games with Pygame, and it is time to put everything we have learned into practice. Over the final two chapters, we are going to use all of our new knowledge to make a space-shooter game. Using our mouse, we're going to control a small but feisty spaceship which will fend off wave after wave of merciless alien hordes, by blasting them with a lethal green laser-ray. In Chapter 10, *The Aliens Are Here and They're Coming in Waves!*, we will also learn how to make levels with organised structures, instead of the random placement of enemies that we will have in this chapter's version of our game.

We'll also add a game-over screen, some UI elements like health and ammunition counters, and we'll add some shields to our space vessel too, because who doesn't like shields?

Since we're not learning anything new this time, we don't need to explore any abstract game or programming concepts before we can make something; we're just going to walk through the code and figure out what we've done and why we've done it that way. So, let's look at the code first, and specifically, at its structure. You may notice that the code for our game is not in one large file as has been the case for most of our previous games. Instead, it has been split across three separate files: one for our main game logic (we've called it **aliens.py**), one that contains the code for our spaceships (**ships.py**), and one file that contains all of the information about our lasers and bullets (**projectiles.py**).

aliens.py is the main program that you should run to start the game. It is responsible for handling how we react to user interactions and game events, such as moving and firing the ship, creating new enemies, and triggering sounds. **ships.py** and **projectiles.py** will be imported by **aliens.py**, and will be used to create our own spaceship, the enemy spaceships, and the projectiles of both of these types of ship.

Aliens.py

Let's break down the structure of **aliens.py** first. This is where everything in the game will start from, so it makes sense that we should too. As in all of our previous programs, we have our import statements at the top. Here, we're importing the modules that we'll need to make our game do its thing. We also import our own file, **ships.py**, which sits in the same folder as **aliens.py**, with `import ship`.

Figure 9-1   The game that we'll make in this half of the tutorial

After the imports, we have all of the usual initialisation, followed by the global variables that we'll use to keep track of the various objects and events that occur in our game. These are 'global' variables because they don't fall within the scope of any function in our program, which means that any functions in our game can read and change the variables as they like. In a lot of circumstances this is frowned upon, but for games it's perfect. Not every variable we need to make this game is declared here; there are quite a few more in our ships and projectile classes which we will get to shortly. Remember, using classes is a great way to keep properties that are relevant to the thing we're using all wrapped up nicely together.

In our variable definitions, we define a couple of image variables for the start screen and the game background, as well as a `Rect` to represent the start button's location on the start screen. After that come game state variables, and a user event that we'll use to spawn new enemies. That's followed by a sprite group we'll use to keep track of all sprites, and an instance of the `Player` object that we store in the variable `ship`. This represents the player's ship. We pass it the variable that represents the main window, as well as the `all_sprites` group. This uses a special version of the sprite constructor that automatically adds the sprite to any group you pass in as an argument.

```python
import pygame
import random
import ships

pygame.init()
pygame.font.init()
clock = pygame.time.Clock()
FPS = 60

WIN_HEIGHT = 614
WIN_WIDTH = 1024
window = pygame.display.set_mode((WIN_WIDTH, WIN_HEIGHT))
pygame.display.set_caption('Aliens Are Gonna Kill Me!')
text_font = pygame.font.SysFont("monospace", 50)
pygame.mixer.init()
start_screen = pygame.image.load("assets/start_screen.png")
background = pygame.image.load("assets/background.png")

# Define the clickable area for the start button
start_button_rect = pygame.Rect(445, 450, 135, 60)
```

```
game_started = False
start_time = 0
time_lasted = 0
NEW_ENEMY = pygame.USEREVENT + 0

all_sprites = pygame.sprite.Group()
ship = ships.Player(window, all_sprites)
```

Next come a couple of short functions. The **add_new_enemy()** function spawns a new enemy ship and then sets a timer that calls this function again. It uses a randomly calculated interval between 1 and 2.5 seconds. Notice that we call the enemy ship constructor, but we don't assign its return value anywhere. That's because we're passing it the **all_sprites** group, and it will be added to that group. Because we track enemy ships as a group, we don't need to store the individual ships anywhere other than the **all_sprites** group. Later on, we'll use the **isinstance()** function to make sure we only operate on members of the group that are enemy ships.

```
def add_new_enemy():
    ships.Enemy(window, 1, all_sprites)
    enemy_interval = random.randint(1000, 2500)
    pygame.time.set_timer(NEW_ENEMY, enemy_interval)

def quit_game():
    pygame.quit()
    raise SystemExit
```

Last, but certainly by no means least, we have our 'main loop'. It checks whether the ESC key was pressed or whether the game window was closed, and if so, calls **quit_game()**. It also checks whether the left mouse button was clicked (by looking for a mouse button up event) and sets the clicked variable to **True** if it's been clicked. When we click the mouse to fire our weapon, we don't want our guns to keep firing for as long as we hold down the button; we want to fire on each click, which is why we look for the **MOUSEBUTTONUP** event rather than **MOUSEBUTTONDOWN** or using **pygame.mouse.get_pressed()**. This way, we can be certain that we only fire once per click, not willy-nilly.

If the timer has triggered the **NEW_ENEMY** event, we call **add_new_enemy()**.

```python
# main loop
while True:

    clicked = False
    # Handle events
    for event in pygame.event.get():
        if event.type == pygame.KEYDOWN:
            if event.key == pygame.K_ESCAPE:
                quit_game()
        if event.type == pygame.MOUSEBUTTONUP:
            if event.button == 1:
                clicked = True

        if event.type == pygame.QUIT:
            quit_game()

        if event.type == NEW_ENEMY:
            add_new_enemy()
```

Next, it stores the mouse position and checks which state we're in. If the game hasn't been started, it shows the start screen and then checks to see if the mouse has been clicked. If so, and if the mouse position overlaps with the start button, we start the game and call **add_new_enemy()** to spawn our first new enemy (which also sets the timer for the next enemy to appear). On the next loop, our game will start: time to kill the alien scourge!

If the game has started and the ship is still alive, we draw the game background, and if the mouse has been clicked, the ship fires a projectile. The ship's position follows the mouse, so we also set the ship's position here. Although we pass the **mouse_position**, which includes the x and y coordinate, to **ship.set_position()**, as you'll see later, we only use the x position. Like many other games in the fixed shooter genre, your ship can only move horizontally.

We then call the sprite group's **update()** method, which calls each sprite's **update()** method, and then we loop through the group, giving each enemy ship the opportunity to fire a weapon, check whether their projectile has hit the player's ship, and check whether their ship's projectiles have hit any enemies. Next, we check to see if the health of the player's ship has dropped to zero or lower, and if so, we log the amount of time that the player survived. Finally, we tell the sprite group to draw all the sprites.

The final state occurs when the ship's health has dropped to zero or less. In that case, we display how long they lasted and exit the game. After proceeding through all those game states, we **tick()** the clock and **update()** the display.

```python
        mouse_position = pygame.mouse.get_pos()

        if not game_started:
            window.blit(start_screen, (0, 0))
            if clicked:
                if start_button_rect.collidepoint(mouse_position):
                    game_started = True
                    start_time = pygame.time.get_ticks()
                    add_new_enemy()

        elif game_started and ship.health > 0:
            window.blit(background, (0, 0))

            if clicked:
                ship.fire()
            ship.set_position(mouse_position)

            all_sprites.update()

            for enemy in all_sprites:
                if isinstance(enemy, ships.Enemy):
                    enemy.try_to_fire()
                    enemy.check_for_hit(ship)
                    ship.check_for_hit(enemy)

            if ship.health <= 0:
                end_time = pygame.time.get_ticks()
                time_lasted = (end_time - start_time) // 1000

            all_sprites.draw(window)
```

```
elif game_started and ship.health <= 0:
    print(f"Game Over! You lasted {time_lasted} seconds.")
    quit_game()

clock.tick(FPS)
pygame.display.update()
```

Ships.py

In the variable declaration section of **aliens.py**, we saw the variable `ship`. This is where we created our player's spaceship. With it, we shall defend the Earth, our solar system and, yes, even the galaxy from the tyranny of all kinds of alien evil! This variable instantiates our `Player` ship class that we imported from our **ships.py** file. If you take a look at **ships.py**, you'll see it's almost as big as **aliens.py**. That should make sense: after all, spaceships are complicated things. In our **ships.py** file, we have two classes: our `Player` class (remember, class names start with a capital letter) and our `Enemy` class. The `Player` class is where all of the logic for moving, firing, drawing, and damaging our own spaceship happens. We also keep track of the sound effects and images used by our spaceship as we play our game.

> **Quick Tip**
>
> The sounds for this tutorial were created using BFXR (**bfxr.net**), a nifty little tool designed for creating sound effects that resemble those from games of times long past. Go and have a play with it!

Figure 9-2   Our ship (left) and an enemy ship (right)

The **init()** method takes care of initialising all the instance variables needed to keep track of your ship. After loading the ship image, we set the ship's position. We're using a different approach than you've seen in the past: first, we take the **midbottom** property from the game window, which corresponds to its centermost x coordinate and its bottommost y coordinate. We subtract 10 from the y coordinate using vector arithmetic, which nudges it up 10 pixels. Next, we pass that as the **midbottom** argument into the **get_rect()** method of the image, which returns a **Rect** that centres the image along the bottom, and then set the player sprite's **rect** property to that **Rect**. When we later call the **draw()** method on the **all_sprites** group, it will use the image and **rect** property to draw each sprite in the game window.

After that, the **init()** method sets the default health, the ship's sound effect, bullet image and bullet speed, and then creates a group just for the ship's bullets and stores the window in an instance variable for later use.

```python
import pygame
import projectiles
import random
from pygame import Vector2

class Player(pygame.sprite.Sprite):

    def __init__(self, win, *groups):
        super().__init__(*groups)

        # Load image and set up sprite
        self.image = pygame.image.load("assets/you_ship.png")
        midbottom = win.get_rect().midbottom - Vector2(0, 10)
        self.rect = self.image.get_rect(midbottom=midbottom)

        # Instance attributes
        self.health = 5
        self.sound_effect = "sounds/player_laser.wav"
        self.bullet_image = "assets/you_pellet.png"
        self.bullet_speed = -10

        self.bullets = pygame.sprite.Group()
        self.window = win
```

The **set_position()** method moves the ship to match where our mouse is. We set the ship's **centerx** property to the x position (first element of the **pos** array), and leave its y position unaltered (like many fixed shooter games such as the venerable Space Invaders, our ship is constrained to move only horizontally).

When we fire our weapon in the **fire()** method, we create a new bullet, and add it to any groups that the ship is part of (it's only a member of **all_sprites**) and the ship's own bullet group. This allows us to keep track of the ship's own bullets. Next, we play a laser sound effect. It may be true that in space no-one can hear you scream, but in *Star Wars* it's infinitely cooler to have blaster sounds going off all around you.

Figure 9-3 Our projectile (top) and the alien projectile (bottom)

Next comes the **check_for_hit()** method, which checks to see whether any of this ship's bullets have hit another ship. If they have, it registers the hit on the other ship by calling **register_hit()** to decrease that ship's health by 1. If that ship's health has dropped to zero or less, **check_for_hit()** calls its **kill()** method, which removes it from any groups that it's part of. Because those groups held the only remaining reference to the ship that was killed, it will eventually be cleaned up by Python's garbage collector.

```
def set_position(self, pos):
    self.rect.centerx = pos[0]
```

```python
def fire(self):
    bullet = projectiles.Bullet(
        self.rect.midtop,
        self.bullet_speed,
        self.bullet_image,
        self.window.get_height()
    )
    bullet.add(self.groups(), self.bullets)

    # Play sound
    sound = pygame.mixer.Sound(self.sound_effect)
    sound.set_volume(0.1)
    sound.play()

def check_for_hit(self, t):
    if pygame.sprite.spritecollide(t, self.bullets, True):
        t.register_hit()

    if t.health <= 0:
        t.kill()

def register_hit(self):
    self.health -= 1
```

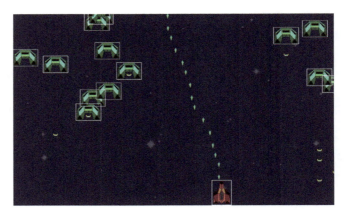

Figure 9-4 The white boxes around our spaceships are a visual representation of collision boundaries

Our **Enemy** class is smaller than our **Player** class. This does not, however, mean it is less complicated. If you look at the class definition for **Enemy**, you'll see we specify the **Player** class as its superclass. When we define a class, if we include the name of another class in its declaration, it will get (inherit) all of the properties and classes of the class that has been passed through. So, **Player** inherits from **Sprite**, and **Enemy** inherits from **Player**. We do this because, despite being on opposite sides of our epic cosmic war of wits and lasers, at its core, a spaceship is a spaceship like any other but with a few tweaks here and there.

So, even though our **Enemy** class doesn't have `fire()`, `register_hit()` and `check_for_hit()` methods typed out, it still has those methods — it just gets them from **Player**. This enables us to use code in different ways across multiple objects, but we can also override some of those methods and add new ones as they're needed for our **Enemy** class. For example, our **Enemy** class has a `try_to_fire()` function. Our **Player** class doesn't have this; only our **Enemy** class does. We can also set different values for the same variables in our **Enemy** class: our `bullet_speed` value in **Enemy** is 10, whereas it's -10 in our **Player** class (the signs are different because they move in different directions). And, of course, the image we're using for each type of ship is different.

Our enemy spaceships aren't that sophisticated when they move: they're hell-bent on our destruction, so they fly straight at us in order to take a potshot. The `update()` method, which is run when we call `all_sprites.update()` in aliens.py, calls the parent class `update()` method first. Even though the parent class (**Player**) doesn't have an `update()` method in ships.py, it inherits it from the **Sprite** class. We're introducing a new function in `update()`: `move_ip()`, which moves the sprite's **rect** *in-place* (without returning a new **Rect** that we'd then have to assign to our **rect**). We pass in the speed vector (0, 2) as an argument, and this moves the enemy ship in the y direction only.

The enemy spaceships will continuously try to take a shot at us. Why 'try'? Well, our enemies are being controlled by Python, which can fire a great deal quicker than you can. `try_to_fire()` is called once per ship in every loop and gives our enemy a 1/100 chance of getting off a shot. That might sound like pretty slim odds for firing at all! But remember, our loop runs 60 times a second, which means that there's a roughly 50-50 chance each enemy will fire a shot every two seconds, so we need to keep our wits about us.

```python
class Enemy(Player):

    def __init__(self, window, *groups):
        super().__init__(window, *groups)

        # Override player-specific attributes
        self.image = pygame.image.load("assets/them_ship.png")
        x_pos = random.randint(0, self.window.get_width())
        self.rect = self.image.get_rect(midtop=(x_pos, -60))

        self.sound_effect = "sounds/enemy_laser.wav"
        self.bullet_image = "assets/them_pellet.png"
        self.bullet_speed = 10
        self.speed = Vector2(0, 2)
        self.health = 1

    def update(self):
        super().update()

        self.rect.move_ip(self.speed)
        if self.rect.y >= self.window.get_height():
            self.kill()

    def try_to_fire(self):
        should_fire = random.random()
        if should_fire <= 0.01:
            self.fire()
```

Projectiles.py

Continuing our use of classes, we have our projectiles **Bullet** class in our **projectiles.py** file. Note that the latter isn't imported into our game in **aliens.py** but in **ships.py**, because our game doesn't need bullets — our ships do. Our **Bullet** class is far simpler than our two ship classes: we have only one method and a range of variables to affect and track each bullet. How do the bullets know when they are hitting something?

Because each bullet created in our game is stored in the **bullets** list in each of our ships, we use the **Player** class method **check_for_hit()** to see whether or not any of the bullets hit anything. There's no real reason for doing it this way — we could have each bullet be responsible for checking if it hit something — but it does make sense to have each ship keep an eye on whether the bullets it fired hit something.

```python
import pygame

class Bullet(pygame.sprite.Sprite):

    def __init__(self, midtop, speed,
                 image_path, window_height):
        super().__init__()

        # Load and set up the image
        self.image = pygame.image.load(image_path)

        # Center the bullet horizontally
        self.rect = self.image.get_rect(midtop=midtop)
        self.velocity = pygame.Vector2(0, speed)
        self.window_height = window_height

    def update(self):
        self.rect.move_ip(self.velocity)

        # Remove bullet if it goes off screen
        if (self.rect.bottom < 0 or
            self.rect.top > self.window_height):

            self.kill()
```

What next?

That's the first half of our game. We don't have much in the way of a game-over screen, so we'll cover making one in our final chapter. We'll program a UI for our health and add shields to our ship. We'll also write some code that will create levels (waves) that you can customise to make each game behave any way you like.

Chapter 10

The Aliens Are Here and They're Coming in Waves!

To wrap up this book, we're going to give the space shooter game we started in the last chapter some extra polish

Welcome to the final chapter! If you have worked this far through the book, you can consider yourself to be quite an expert in building games with Pygame. We are going to round things off by adding a final polish to the space shooter game we began in the last chapter.

If you look over the code from the previous chapter and compare it to the code for this one, you'll see that, despite having the same foundations, there's quite a bit more going on this time around. Previously, we dealt with creating a start screen, moving our ship, firing our weapons, creating enemies, having them fire their weapons, and then removing them from time and space whenever we hit one another. Now, we are going to enrich our game by adding shields to our spaceship and create a simple health/shield bar to show their status. We're also going to write some code that lets us create levels and waves for our enemy spaceships to fall into, as well as writing some logic for announcing that the next level of bad guys is on its way. Finally, we'll create two end screens: one for if the aliens kill us, another for if we survive all of the levels of the onslaught.

A tour at warp speed

We've seen most of this code before, obviously, but a good deal has changed. We're not going to show the code in its entirety in this chapter, so we'll look at just the parts that have changed. As with previous chapters, you can download the code and assets from the GitHub repository at **rpimag.co/pygamebookgit**.

> **Quick Tip**
>
> If you know how to use a file difference tool such as the command-line diff utility, comparing this chapter's code with the previous chapter's will help you get a complete oversight of what we've changed and why.

Let's begin with **aliens.py**. We now import another file, **gamelevels.py**. This file contains a list with a number of dictionaries which we'll use to place our enemies in the different levels of our game. It's a big file, but it's not a complicated one, and we'll take a look at it shortly. We don't need the `random` module in **aliens.py**, so we've removed that `import`.

```
import pygame
import ships
import gamelevels
```

We also have some new variables. We will use these to keep track of our game's progress and state, as well as changing levels. We also load a couple of extra images to use in our game; these will be our game over and wave announcement graphics.

We've done away with the `start_time` and `time_lasted` variables, and we've renamed the `NEW_ENEMY` user-defined event to `NEW_WAVE`. We've also added another user-defined event, `CLEAR_NEXT_LEVEL_MSG`, which we'll use to indicate when it's time to remove the incoming wave message.

```
incoming_wave = pygame.image.load("assets/next_level.png")
win_screen = pygame.image.load("assets/win_screen.png")
lose_screen = pygame.image.load("assets/lose_screen.png")
last_lvl_screen = pygame.image.load("assets/final_level.png")
# Define the clickable area for the start button
start_button_rect = pygame.Rect(445, 450, 135, 60)
```

```
game_started = False
curr_lvl = 0
curr_wave = 0
show_msg = False
game_won = False
last_lvl = False
NEW_WAVE = pygame.USEREVENT + 0
CLEAR_NEXT_LEVEL_MSG = pygame.USEREVENT + 1
```

Let's take a look at a matrix

The biggest change in this version of our game is that we can now define levels and formations for our enemy ships to attack us with. If you take a look at **gamelevels.py**, you'll see there is only one variable, `level`. We're not going to show the file here, but you can find it in the GitHub repository.

The `level` variable is an array of dictionaries that contains objects which describe our levels. Our first level or 'wave' is the first dictionary, the second level is the second dictionary, and so on. Each `level` dictionary has two properties: `interval` and `structure`. Let's take a look at the `structure` property first: this is a list of lists, and in each list is a series of 1s and 0s. Each list is a wave. Think of `structure` as a map of our game window. The width of our game window is represented by one list inside of `structure`. For each 1 in our list, we want to create an enemy spaceship in corresponding space in our game window, and for every 0 we don't. Using this approach, we can define levels of different difficulty and appearance, just by changing the values of `structure`. For example, if we wanted to create ten ships that spanned the width of the screen at equal intervals, we'd add a list like this to our `structure` list:

```
[1,1,1,1,1,1,1,1,1,1]
```

If we wanted that row of ships to be followed by a row of six ships with a gap in the middle, we'd add two lists to `structure`, one for the first row of spaceships, and another for the second:

```
[1,1,1,1,1,1,1,1,1,1],
[1,1,1,0,0,0,0,1,1,1]
```

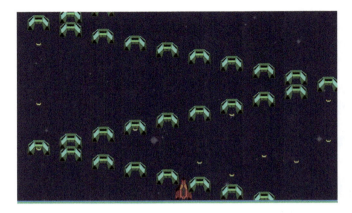

Figure 10-1 By adjusting patterns and intervals, you can make unique levels

This structure is known as a *matrix*, which you can think of as a list with an X and Y axis. If you wanted to know whether or not we were going to create a spaceship in the second grid down from the top of the matrix (which corresponds to the level's second wave) and three across, you could check with `level[0]["structure"][1][2]`, but that's not quite how we're using this in our game. However, remember that Python arrays are zero-indexed, so the second element of an array has index 1, and the third has index 2.

The other property of our `level` objects is `interval`. This value sets how many seconds should pass before we move on from one wave and create the next. Tweaking this value can greatly change the difficulty of each level. For example, if you have five waves of enemies with a five-second interval between each row, you'll have ten spaceships being generated every five seconds that you need to destroy. That's quite a lot, but 50 enemies over 25 seconds is pretty easy to deal with. However, if you create ten rows of ships and set the interval between waves to two seconds, you're going to be dealing with 100 ships in 20 seconds. That really is an onslaught!

To illustrate this, the final level included in **gamelevels.py** contains five times the number of waves than any other level, but there is only one ship in each wave and the interval is 0.5 seconds. This creates a zigzag pattern of ships, which makes for interesting gameplay when you're being fired at by ships across both the X and Y axes. With this knowledge, you can create a limitless variety of levels for our game; all you have to do is copy one of the level objects and edit the structure and interval as you see fit. That's much more fun than spawning enemies at random X/Y coordinates.

Figure 10-2 We can determine enemy spaceship positions using a matrix

Launch wave!

Now that we know how to structure our levels, how do we put them together in our game? In **aliens.py** we have the **add_new_wave()** function. This generates enemies at the correct positions and correct time for the current level and wave. At the end of the function, we set a timer based on the interval value for the current level we're playing; when the timer event fires, **add_new_wave()** is called again.

The first thing **launchWave()** does is create the variable **this_level**. We don't absolutely have to do this, but it makes what we're trying to do a little more obvious when we access our level structure, rather than typing out **gameLevels.level[curr_lvl]["structure"]** every time. Next, we check that the wave we're about to create actually exists in our level. If our level has four waves and we try to access a fifth one, our game will crash. If the wave we want to access does exist, we take that wave and assign it to the **wave** variable. Again, this just makes our code a little nicer to read. We then work through the values of that wave by running a **for** loop over the result of the **enumerate()** function, which returns both the array index (**idx**) and value (**enemy**) of each array element.

If **enemy** is 1, we place an alien, if not, we don't. If we do, we then call the **Enemy()** constructor, but we've added two new arguments: **idx** and the length of the wave (number of elements in this wave's array). The constructor will use these values to work out where to place the enemy.

Once **launchWave()** has created the enemies it needs to, it increments **curr_wave** and lets the game continue on its way until it is called by our main loop again. If the next time **launchWave()** is run, it finds that there are no more waves in this level, it will check to see if there's another level it can move on to. If so, it will recharge our ship's shields, increase the level number, and reset the wave number to 0. New level!

If **launchWave()** finds that it's run out of waves to create and that there aren't any more levels to play, it sets the **game_won** variable to **True**. This is a preliminary value, as nothing will happen until all of the enemies have been destroyed, either by our bodacious laser blasts or by them simply flying off the screen to their oblivion. If we survive all of the levels and aren't destroyed by a lucky potshot from one of our alien foes, then we've won the game! Hurrah!

```python
def add_new_wave():
    global curr_lvl, curr_wave, show_msg, game_won, last_lvl

    this_level = gamelevels.level[curr_lvl]["structure"]
    if curr_wave < len(this_level):
        wave = this_level[curr_wave]
        for idx, enemy in enumerate(wave):
            if enemy:
                ships.Enemy(window, idx,
                            len(wave), all_sprites)
        curr_wave += 1

    elif curr_lvl + 1 < len(gamelevels.level):
        curr_lvl += 1
        curr_wave = 0
        ship.shield = ship.MAX_SHIELD
        show_msg = True
        pygame.time.set_timer(CLEAR_NEXT_LEVEL_MSG, 5000)
        if curr_lvl == len(gamelevels.level) - 1:
            last_lvl = True

    else:
```

```
        game_won = True

        delay = gamelevels.level[curr_lvl]["interval"] * 1000
        pygame.time.set_timer(NEW_WAVE, delay)
```

We've got another new function in **aliens.py**, **reset_game()**. This is used to start a new game after winning or losing. It sets all the game variables back to their default state, resets the ship's health and shields, and adds it to the **all_sprites** group. You may remember that when a ship's health drops to zero, it's removed from all groups with the **kill()** function. For every other sprite in the game, this is their end, because the only reference to them is from a sprite group. However, in **aliens.py**, we have the **ship** variable, which means the ship still exists, at least from Python's perspective. At the end of the function, we call **add_new_wave()** to set up the first incoming wave of enemies.

```
def reset_game():
    global game_won, curr_lvl, curr_wave, show_msg, last_lvl

    game_won = False
    curr_lvl = 0
    curr_wave = 0
    show_msg = False
    last_lvl = False

    # Add the ship back to the sprites group.
    all_sprites.add(ship)
    ship.health = ship.MAX_HEALTH
    ship.shield = ship.MAX_SHIELD
    add_new_wave()
```

In the **aliens.py** main loop, we've made a few other changes. Because we've renamed the **NEW_ENEMY** event to **NEW_WAVE**, we need to look for that event and call **add_new_wave()**. We also have a new key press to look for: the **SPACE** key. That's because our game end screens prompt the player (win or lose) to press **SPACE** to start a new game.

We also have to look for the **CLEAR_NEXT_LEVEL_MSG** event and set **show_msg** to **False** if it's triggered (this is how we limit the amount of time the message is displayed).

```
    for event in pygame.event.get():
        if event.type == pygame.KEYDOWN:
            if event.key == pygame.K_ESCAPE:
                quit_game()
            if event.key == pygame.K_SPACE:
                if game_won or ship.health <= 0:
                    reset_game()
        if event.type == NEW_WAVE:
            add_new_wave()
        if event.type == CLEAR_NEXT_LEVEL_MSG:
            show_msg = False
        if event.type == pygame.MOUSEBUTTONUP:
            if event.button == 1:
                clicked = True
        if event.type == pygame.QUIT:
            quit_game()
```

Within the **if/elif** statement that determines what do to in the current game state, we have a few small changes. First, in the **if not game_started** part, we call **add_new_wave()** instead of **add_new_enemy()**.

The second state of the game is the one in which **game_started** is **True** and the ship's health is greater than 0. We have to add another condition to that (**and not game_won**), and also display a message if **show_msg** is **True**: if we're on the last level, we display a special last level message, otherwise we just show a warning that a new wave is imminent. At the end of this section, we draw the shield and health meter on screen:

```
    elif game_started and ship.health > 0 and not game_won:
        window.blit(background, (0, 0))
        if show_msg:
            if last_lvl:
                window.blit(last_lvl_screen, (250, 150))
            else:
                window.blit(incoming_wave, (250, 150))

        # unchanged code has been omitted

        window.blit(ship.shield_meter(), (0, WIN_HEIGHT - 5))
        window.blit(ship.health_meter(), (0, WIN_HEIGHT - 10))
```

The last change to **aliens.py** is the introduction of two new game states: when the game is lost and when it's won. We display the appropriate screen and remove all the sprites from the `all_sprites` group, which makes them all (with the exception of `ship`) eligible to be cleaned up the next time Python's garbage collector runs.

```
elif game_started and ship.health <= 0:
    window.blit(lose_screen, (0, 0))
    all_sprites.empty()

elif game_started and game_won:
    window.blit(win_screen, (0, 0))
    all_sprites.empty()
```

> **Quick Tip**
>
> Just because you're following a tutorial, it doesn't mean you have to use all of the resources we provide. Why not tweak some of the images to create your own unique spaceship? Or mess around with the level structures and ships classes to create more than one enemy ship? Learning comes from trying these things out and seeing how far you get!

Full power to the forward deflector shields!

What does every spaceship need? Obviously, it has to have energy shields to keep it safe from cosmic dust and enemy fire alike.

Implementing shields for our ship is not particularly difficult. We did most of the work already when we created health for our ships. At the top of the `Player` class, we define three new global variables, which we'll use later.

```
MAX_HEALTH = 5
MAX_SHIELD = 3
HEALTH_COLOURS = [(62, 180, 76), (180, 62, 62)]
```

In its `init()` constructor, we're loading a second image (`shield_img`), a transparent PNG that we draw over our ship when it's been hit, to give a cool bit of feedback to our players. We're also loading our ship image into the `ship_img` property and setting our image property to a copy of the ship image. If we didn't make a copy, we'd inadvertently modify the original ship image when we draw over it in the upcoming **update()** method.

```
self.ship_img = pygame.image.load(
    "assets/you_ship.png")
self.shield_img = pygame.image.load(
    "assets/shield1.png")
self.image = self.ship_img.copy()
```

You have two choices for your shield shape: a bubble shield (**shield1.png**), like the USS Enterprise has, or a shape shield (**shield2.png**), like those found in *Stargate*. You can change them by loading the image you prefer (see **Figure 10-3**).

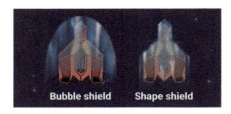

Figure 10-3   The two different shields

We make a couple of other changes in the constructor: we set **health** to **MAX_HEALTH**, add the new **shield** property and set it to **MAX_SHIELD**. Finally, we add a **last_hit** property to keep track of how long ago the ship was hit.

```
self.health = self.MAX_HEALTH
self.shield = self.MAX_SHIELD
self.last_hit = 0
```

The **update()** method is new. In the last chapter, **Player** didn't have its own **update()** method — it merely inherited it from its parent class, **Sprite**. In this method, we first call the parent class **update()** method, and then we fill the ship's image with a transparent background (although we specify black with 0, 0, 0, we set the alpha channel to 0, which makes it completely transparent). This is because we need to redraw the ship image when the shields are active. To do this, we first **blit()** the default ship image over the **image** property. Next, we check to see if our **last_hit** time is greater than zero. If it is, and if it's been less than 250 milliseconds since we were hit, we **blit()** the shield image over it. Because the shield image has transparency, it doesn't completely obscure the ship itself.

Because classes inherit from one another, **Enemy**'s **update()** method will call this one. However, you'll see that we set the enemy's shield value to 0, so we'll never draw a shield image over an enemy.

```python
def update(self):
    super().update()
    self.image.fill((0, 0, 0, 0))
    self.image.blit(self.ship_img, (0, 0))
    if self.last_hit > 0 and self.shield > 0:
        elapsed = pygame.time.get_ticks() - self.last_hit
        if elapsed < 250:
            self.image.blit(self.shield_img, (-3, -2))
```

Previously, our **register_hit()** method would decrease our health value by 1 until it was 0. Now, it will check if we have any shield energy left; if our shield levels are greater than 0, we'll decrement the shield level instead of the health level. If our shields are at 0, then we decrease the health value just like we did before. We'll also set the **last_hit** property so we know how long to draw a shield overlay.

```python
def register_hit(self):
    if self.shield <= 0:
        self.health -= 1
    else:
        self.shield -= 1
    self.last_hit = pygame.time.get_ticks()
```

While we're on the subject of shields and health, let's look at how we create health and shield bars. Back in **aliens.py**, we called the ship's **shield_meter()** and **health_meter()** methods and drew the result on screen. These methods are relatively simple: they create a surface that's five pixels high — its width is scaled according to the percentage of shields or health remaining. For example, if we can sustain three more hits, the health bar will be full across the width of our game screen; if it can take two hits, it will fill two-thirds of the screen, and so on until it is empty.

For the shields, it's always drawn in the same (tealish) colour, but the health meter is drawn in green until it drops down to 1, in which case it's drawn in red so as to induce the appropriate amount of stress and nervous tension.

```python
def shield_meter(self):
    percent = self.shield / self.MAX_SHIELD
    s = Surface((percent * self.window.get_width(), 5))
    s.fill((62, 145, 180))
    return s

def health_meter(self):
    percent = self.health / self.MAX_HEALTH
    s = Surface((percent * self.window.get_width(), 5))
    if self.health <= 1:
        which_colour = self.HEALTH_COLOURS[1]
    else:
        which_colour = self.HEALTH_COLOURS[0]
    s.fill(which_colour)
    return s
```

The **Enemy** class has not changed too much. Because the parent class (**Player**) **update()** method draws the **ship_img** into the ship's **image** property, we need to define that and copy it into the image just as we did in **Player**'s **init()**. We also need to do a little bit of maths to work out where to place each enemy. First, we divide the window width by the length of the list that makes up the wave; we then place the ship at the X coordinate that is equal to the window width divided by the number of slots in the wave multiplied by the index of this enemy.

So, if we have ten slots in this wave, the **launch_wave()** function in **aliens.py** will pass in 10 as the **len** argument. If we're currently working on the second enemy in the wave, **idx** will be equal to 1 (remember, Python arrays are zero-indexed). With a window width of 1024, the second enemy's middle top x coordinate would be **(1024 / 10) * 1**, or 102. (See **Figure 10-4**)

```python
# Override player-specific attributes
self.ship_img = pygame.image.load(
    "assets/them_ship.png")
```

```
self.image = self.ship_img.copy()

x_pos = (window.get_width() // len) * idx
self.rect = self.image.get_rect(midtop=(x_pos, -60))
```

We've also made a couple of smaller changes: we've made the enemies a little faster by setting the y component of their **speed** vector to 4, and we've also added a **shield** property and set it to 0.

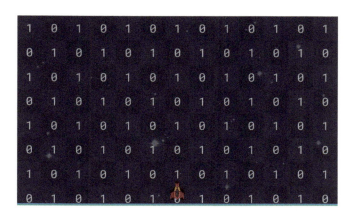

Figure 10-4 Mapping the matrix to the dimensions of our game window

That's all, folks!

And that's it: we're finished! You should now be able to go out into the world and make simple video games using Python and Pygame. Let's quickly go through all of the things we've learned over the course of this volume. We've learned how to draw basic shapes; how to use a keyboard and mouse to move, create, and delete things; we've learned all about gravity (or at least, a super-simple version of it); we've learned how to bounce things off of other things and how to register things hitting one another; we've learned all about playing sounds and blitting images; and tons and tons of stuff about Pygame and system events. We've also learned that Python is straightforward, and ideal for getting up and going from scratch, for beginners and experts alike. We hope you have enjoyed learning all these new skills, and are looking forward to putting them into practice. Have fun!